ghost dance

ghost dance

Douglas Wright

PENGUIN BOOKS

PENGUIN BOOKS
Published by the Penguin Group
Penguin Books (NZ) Ltd, cnr Airborne and Rosedale Roads, Albany,
Auckland 1310, New Zealand
Penguin Books Ltd, 80 Strand, London, WC2R 0RL, England
Penguin Group (USA) Inc., 375 Hudson Street, New York, NY 10014, United States
Penguin Books Australia Ltd, 250 Camberwell Road, Camberwell,
Victoria 3124, Australia
Penguin Books Canada Ltd, 10 Alcorn Avenue, Toronto,
Ontario, Canada M4V 3B2
Penguin Books (South Africa) (Pty) Ltd, 24 Sturdee Avenue, Rosebank,
Johannesburg 2196, South Africa
Penguin Books India (P) Ltd, 11, Community Centre, Panchsheel Park,
New Delhi 110 017, India
Penguin Books Ltd, Registered Offices: 80 Strand, London, WC2R 0RL, England

First published by Penguin Books (NZ) Ltd, 2004
1 3 5 7 9 10 8 6 4 2

Designed by Mary Egan
Typeset by Egan-Reid Ltd
Editorial services by Michael Gifkins & Associates
Printed in Australia by McPherson's Printing Group

The poem on page 74 is from *Living in the Maniototo* by Janet Frame.

ISBN 0 14 301903 1
A catalogue record for this book is available
from the National Library of New Zealand.

www.penguin.co.nz

Contents

... [a person] circumnambulates Mount Kailash by performing body-length prostrations. One round of Kailash is about 52 kilometres (32 miles) and takes two weeks to complete in this way. The circuit includes snow-covered mountain paths that rise to 5,636 metres (18,500 feet). Pilgrims come to Kailash to atone for their sins and to ensure they are reborn in the human world, rather than in hell or as hungry ghosts.

Once pilgrims start doing prostrations they cannot take any short cuts or skip any difficult sections of the route, such as icy streams or frozen ground. The greater the suffering the greater the merit gained. Prostrating requires great strength, so mostly young men perform such devotions.

from *Tibet* by KAZUYOSHI NOMACHI

Joys impregnate. Sorrows bring forth.

WILLIAM BLAKE

for Malcolm

Author's note

ghost dance is not a conventional autobiography with a linear progression through one life, but a faithful record of the journeys I felt compelled to make into my own past and that of a close friend. The appointments I kept and the discoveries I made took on their own shape, in the telling, and by the time I finally let go of my preconceptions as to what a book such as mine should be like, the last words were falling into place.

Part One

– 1 –

Invalid

It was after more than a decade of living with a disease once thought fatal I began to suspect that somehow, somewhere along the way, without noticing it, I had already died. In the early days of this post-modern plague people died in almost festive droves, some of them my friends and lovers. For years I felt we were climbing, in single file, a steep and narrow staircase which led to a platform over a bottom-less pit, and we were being pressed so hard from behind that once at the front you had no choice but to jump or be pushed. Then gradual advances in science helped create a generation that could, with luck, we were told, live a nearly normal life. Some of us had already been half-killed by a combination of the illness itself and the poisons we were fed to cure it. The slow-breaking news of my possible reprieve caused me to begin, perversely, to secretly mourn a death I felt cheated of. The sword that still hung by a hair over my head was put on hold as I began to eke out an existence in a kind of limbo.

Over the years, one by one, many of my remaining friends fell away. The initial glamour of being close to someone with a terminal, fashionable illness gave way, in some cases to a barely concealed impatience. Increasingly irritable, constantly tired, hungry for solitude, I began to refuse invitations. Face-to-face conversations with the rudely healthy felt at times like being gnawed at by rats. Because the disease was communicable, I ruled out sex. No longer touching or being touched, I became extremely touchy. I longed for insults, any excuse to narrow my circle of friends. Those that remained were hardy; survivors of all kinds of misfortune and disease, the walking wounded, foetal saints. Sometimes, for fun, we laughed ourselves sick. We were there for each other. But where 'there' actually was increasingly mystified me as I spent more and more time alone. For twenty years I had been a dancer and choreographer but after a series of ill-fated projects, each one more harrowing than its predecessor, I had reached the end of my tether.

My mother and I spoke on the phone every night. Sometimes in the middle of a sentence Mum would cry out, 'Get down you naughty thing,' or, 'Yoooouuuu stop that, leave her alone!' and even though I knew she was talking to her cats, I was always taken aback. She, the 'cat's mother', was, like me, recently retired and found time weighed on her hands. So she kept herself busy and once started on something, couldn't stop until it was finished. It was an obsession she got from Granddad and passed on to me. Mum said, 'You don't get it from the ground, you know.' We told each other wonderingly the lengths we went to not to let the sun go down on an unfinished task.

Her latest project was unravelling and re-knitting in a smaller size a cardigan that had got too big for her. It worried me my mother was, apparently, shrinking.

I lived in a pale blue state-owned unit in a quiet suburb of Auckland with a fat black cat, a palm garden and walls of books. An army of pills kept me, to all intents and purposes, alive. These pills had side-effects. To put it mildly. Warren, an ex-boyfriend, was the one in a million recipient of side-effects so severe they killed him. His death raised the question of when does a side-effect become central?

My own experience by comparison was gentle; years of ecstatic diarrhoea, constant gnawing headaches and other, more bizarre effects. One course of drugs included white pills the size of hockey pucks, ground up and choked down with a glass of water at dawn and dusk. This regime caused the fat on my body to gradually migrate from my arms, legs, face, and buttocks to settle around my middle. After eighteen months, although my doctor was thrilled with my bloods, I looked like a pregnant stick-figure, or someone with mal-nutrition. People I hardly knew rushed to give me the news that my bottom had disappeared. Another friend developed a prominent widow's hump of fatty flesh which everybody looked at but nobody mentioned. It was somehow dromedary, stored-up nutrition for the coming expedition into a cruel desert and I was puzzled as to why the disappearance of buttocks invited comment and the appearance of humps didn't. When I stopped this course of treatment I had to wonder if I would be prepared to die of vanity.

Another pill with a name I can never remember, a name that sounds like a concentration camp for Martians, had the peculiar side-effect of inducing temporary psychosis. I was warned to take it just before I went to sleep and told I may be troubled by weird, vivid dreams for the first week or two. That night I woke as usual with a full bladder at about 2 a.m. to find that my head was peopled with a chorus of voices busily commenting on my every movement. They were incensed, thrilled, outraged and astonished by my predicament. I found if I lay very still they subsided into low mutterings and sub-verbal expressions of interest in my next move, but every time I so much as even thought of getting up they broke at once into squawks of abuse.

In my state-owned unit, with my fat black cat watching, in the middle of the night, my blood froze. Like Gulliver pinned to the ground by a horde of schizophrenic Lilliputians. Like someone about to throw themselves off a tall building just to stop the voices.

It was soon after that I began to doubt whether I really was still in the land of the living. I took to walking, for exercise, to get out and about, and on my daily walks around Auckland I began to notice things – splashes of paint on the pavement, squashed chewing-gum, the movements of abandoned plastic bags or torn, crumpled leaves of newspaper in the wind; all the haphazard markings and writhings seemed to beckon to me, to dance in my mind, demanding to be understood.

And the people. Beneath notice, the unloved, unwashed, un-housed and unseen garbage-eaters started looking at me as if they knew me from somewhere, as if I was one of them. One person who resembled a famous local painter strode around in an old grey overcoat with a dishevelled face. As I passed him one day he stage-whispered, 'Dancer!' Another, an ex drag-queen who I knew for a fact had been run over and killed three months previously, broke into a mocking, deadpan skip as she passed me, a knowing glint in her eye.

Thirty years before I had slept with her gypsy boyfriend.

And so on.

The government of the time was relatively maternal and in due course a series of mournful, plump-buttocked Polynesian civil servants respectfully guided me over the bureaucratic hurdles necessary before I was granted an Invalid's Benefit. Then from my cosy position suckling at the iron breast I saw my past spread out in front of me as if it was the future, and my future, magically, became a thing of the past.

– 2 –

Raptor

As I looked out over the landscape of my personal history I found that wherever I directed my attention, something was blocking the view. At first I thought there was a mote of dust in my eye, a black spot, or one of those visual disturbances that can signal the onset of cataracts or blindness, but then I realised it was a person, someone I knew standing there, and after several failed attempts to go around or simply ignore him I finally realised the only way into my past was through his. This alarming discovery was the culmination of a series of inklings that began almost two years before.

In November 2001, I travelled to Dunedin in the South Island to do some research for *Inland*, a dance-theatre work I was planning. Malcolm, my ex-lover and close friend, agreed to fly down from his home up north to meet me for a few days of sightseeing. For reasons never entirely clear to me, he had reached the age of fifty without ever leaving the North Island of New Zealand, so this was to be his first trip 'overseas'. Malcolm had always encouraged me to tell him stories about my childhood and family, claiming his own were so distant and barren that my family's reckless excesses and passionate feuds were things he had been deprived of. He often said, 'I love your family,' and although I couldn't see why, I was so drunk with the power of the one who is listened to that I paid scant attention to the scraps and hints of his own story he occasionally let slip. Though a gifted artist, he steadfastly refused to exhibit, and while his less-talented contemporaries sank to varying degrees of fame and power, he moved into a life of beleaguered anonymity. Prey to all kinds of worries he took to drink, and from time to time I feared he had been inflicted with wounds so deep he may not survive.

One morning soon after Malcolm arrived we got on a red bus just outside our motel in St Kilda and rode into the city to pick up our rental car. After a long search we found the car-rental office where it was hiding to be told by the woman behind the counter that due to a mix-up our vehicle would not be ready for at least an hour, so could we come back then? As Malcolm drifted out backwards for 'a fag', I said, 'No, I'll wait,' and sat down as close to the woman as I could get and proceeded first to turn myself into stone and then to exude a thick black cloud of anger. This performance was so successful that by some miracle a car was made available within less than five minutes and I gratefully turned myself back into flesh and dispelled the black cloud with smiles all round. Actually the woman seemed almost pleased. She was a good sport and waved cheerfully as we drove off through a light drizzling mist in search of the famed Otago landscape.

Gradually the houses, the cars, the people, then even the trees fell away, until we were driving through a windscoured emptiness of such stark beauty that we were dumbstruck and the last traces of my black mood disappeared. It was clear that, in terms of moodiness, the landscape outdid me. The hills were so attenuated and grave they were like the visual equivalent of the opening theme in a Bach fugue, slowed down by years. As their rhythm deepened, the dark, low-hanging curtain of mist lifted slightly, sounding a note of muted colour: white, iron grey, sullen brown, and the blackest black in blackdom. When the horizon was just one long in-held breath, a ray of light thrust its arm through the clouds and painted a fleeting patch a kind of venomous green. The whole space seemed to ring with a strict joy, like the last metallic shivers of a struck bell. It was as if some vengeful God had just left.

As we drove further into the emptiness the name 'McCahon' started to float in the air between us like a speech-balloon. Colin McCahon, Malcolm's ex-teacher, had painted this landscape. He saw an angel here and said, 'Angels can herald beginnings.' The absolute simplicity of these works had seemed to me an abstraction until now. Now I saw he painted what was here and by the accuracy of his vision had claimed it. His legendary bitterness at the initial and prolonged rejection of his work and his utter refusal to compromise were qualities he shared with this battle-scarred landscape, qualities he had passed on, like an infection, to Malcolm. But McCahon had won his battle and I kept expecting to see his signature and the date written in the bottom left-hand corner somewhere. And yet there was no corner, and I realised that although from our point of view the hills were solid and still, from another perspective the land was always moving, with different layers, currents and undertows swelling, colliding and crashing in ever-changing formations. Tongues of ice spoke then withdrew, what was underneath for millions of years was exhumed, mountains rolled over in their flooded plains and rivers wriggled to the sea like frightened snakes. And above all this the eternal wind and rain kept driving the creeping earth from place to place in herds so infinitesimal we couldn't even see them. We were the merest ghost of a blip in a film that might never end and, from this perspective at least, McCahon had written his name on the bottom left-hand corner of the wind.

I stopped the car and we got out, climbed a fence and, leaning into the gale, walked towards an outcrop of schist. Being inside the car had given me no idea of the power of the biting wind. Now I felt as if it was blowing right through me and if I stood there long enough, it would devour me. We took out our cameras and photographed the hills and the sky and the flattened remains of a dead lamb that looked like a fluffy white flower that had been pressed between the wintry pages of a large book. Definitely the Bible. Old Testament. Then we each tried to find a private spot to pee, but there was nothing to hide behind so we peed anyway, careful in case it blew back in our faces.

As we continued inland we suddenly entered a kind of moonscape. The constant attrition and upthrust of hidden deformities had removed most of the surface flesh, exposing more and more of the obstinate bone beneath. These rapidly multiplying outcrops of schist seemed to rush at us as we drove through them, in shapes Aztec, heliolithic, the pulverised ruins of a giant insect cult or perhaps even the shattered skeleton of the insect itself. One of the largish rocks had painted on its overhang in tall white letters in either a homage to, or a parody of, McCahon's later word paintings. We couldn't decide which, agreeing there was a faint possibility the writer was the kind of genuine religious graffitist McCahon was indebted to.

Then, just as suddenly, we left the outcrops behind (or rather they allowed us to escape) and the small town of Middlemarch came into view. We had been warned by the woman at the car rental office that the folks at the general store in Middlemarch may not serve us as we were so obviously 'not of the area'. Our expectations raised, we were disappointed when the admittedly reserved man behind the counter made us tea and sandwiches without so much as a token rudeness. Though when I think back, I'm sure I detected a wild, inbred look in his eye as he asked us if we wanted milk and sugar.

Before we set out, on account of my condition, we agreed to only go as far as Middlemarch so we then turned around and drove back

to Dunedin, leaving the rest of the Bach fugue for another day. On the return journey we saw everything in reverse order and from the back, stopping once to photograph the graffiti-inscribed rock and then just as we were re-entering the emptiness I saw a hawk huddled over roadkill in the middle of the road. I slowed the car and the raptor looked up from its feast like a disgruntled vampire surprised in mid-suck, spread its wings and began to beat them. It rose above its prey but then faltered and Malcolm and I both noticed at the same time that its talons were caught in the squashed corpse which in turn was glued by its own juices to the tarsealed road. I stopped the car as the trapped bird struggled to free itself and just as we were getting out, cameras poised, it broke loose and for an instant too immanent to photograph, the bird hovered, powerful wings beating, right in front of us. Its eyes glittering and its beak bloodied it gave us an insolent, Nosferatu look, ascended swiftly into the air, then vanished.

When we got back to our motel unit across from St Kilda beach Malcolm and I looked up the hawk in my new book, *Maori Bird Lore* by Murdoch Riley. I was planning to use large video-projections of this native hawk in my forthcoming work so our sighting seemed auspicious. The entry was long and contained some essential information:

> Common name: HARRIER
> *circus approximans*
> Common Maori Names: KAHU, KERANGI
> '... the harrier was long regarded by tohunga and the people as being a messenger to and from the gods ... in other accounts described as the offspring of Mahuika, goddess of fire. It is said from this ancestry comes the reddish-brown colour of the under parts of the harrier, i.e. "The red feathers of that bird resembled the seeds of flame."'

We were both exhilarated by the day with its 'seeds of flame', and as we pored over the book together I remembered Malcolm had been an obsessive bird-watcher when he was a boy.

– 3 –

Mapping nests

Worst-case scenario, Malcolm was born on Black Friday, possibly Easter Sunday, definitely April the thirteenth. At times his steps seem so dogged with misfortune he reminds me of a man who has broken a forest of mirrors, walked under a city of ladders, opened a flock of bat-winged umbrellas inside houses while black cats ran back and forth perpetually across his path. He chain-smokes and like one of Beckett's bleak, self-denigrating tramps, sometimes almost chokes to death laughing at his own bad jokes. He has such a generous aversion to himself he extends it to others, then wants it back. In fact he does everything backwards, hugging the people he loves so hard it hurts them while being excessively polite and deferential to those he despises. Like all good Christians he seeks out pain, is nervous of pleasure and is currently serving a life-sentence for an unspeakable crime he never committed. Feral children raised by she-wolves display a similar aversion when confronted with such things as clothes and furniture. There are tribes of people who believe sitting on a chair will make you sick; they know white civilisation is a virus. Malcolm has something of the hawk about him, with the short end of a snapped wishbone behind his radar eyes, and not surprisingly for a self-destructive birdman, he loves cats. One of his favourite things is to listen to the dumb stories I make up as to why my black cat Leo decided to do this or that. Whenever he sees a cat he makes a little clicking noise with his mouth and they either roll over on their backs for their stomachs to be scratched or stalk off in high dudgeon at his impudence. That's when he puts his hand up to cover his rotting teeth and laughs. And every now and then he makes or says or does something that hits the bull's-eye, like the time he saved my life by asking me a question.

Malcolm is obsessed with his parents and what they did to him. Even though they're both now dead he still holds them accountable, like a litigious necromancer. His childhood seems lodged under his skin; a thorn or splinter gone septic. That day, in the motel room in St Kilda, I was too tired to ask him about his childhood bird-watching and it wasn't until months later I finally got around to it. We were sitting on my balcony on a sunny day in early spring, with my cactus collection bristling and poking up around us and a choir of birds singing excitedly in the background. As he talked Malcolm chain-smoked and punctuated his words with a flurry of gestures that made him look as if he was selecting and wielding delicate instruments.

In the 1950s and 60s his father was a sole-charge teacher in the Maori Schools Service and his mother was a missionary historian.

Although both atheists, they worshipped the God of Reason and when Malcolm was diagnosed as a backward reader in his first year at school, his father was outraged. As a pre-schooler Malcolm had a fetish for snapdragons, and a fascination with drawing, but words, to him, were mysterious. One at a time he could almost grasp them, but in regiments, with his father as their screaming general, they became incomprehensible, and all his father's biffs and clouts only made him long to be invisible. Out of nowhere it was biff, clout and then a backhander. Biff, clout and then a backhander. And the shouting and screaming.

His older brother, by way of contrast, was extremely good with numbers. The family moved a lot. As Malcolm described it, it was as if they were on a long sea-journey in a church-shaped ship with his father at the helm and his mother keeping the logbook and they were sailing towards a brave new world that was imaginary. By the time

he was six they were living in the isolated hamlet of Motukiore Creek. It was a Maori community; Malcolm's family, the Rosses, and a poor white family called the Shepherds, were the only Pakeha in the area and despite all good intentions his father was the squire and the Maori were the peasants. Malcolm's attempts at insignificance failed miserably. The smaller he did things, the more they stuck out. He became a whole tribe of cringing defects for his parents to correct. While his mother used words and silence, his father committed violence in his official capacity as Malcolm's teacher. Once, in front of the class, he grabbed Malcolm by the wrist and swung him face-first into the wall. To help with his spelling. The school-house was only fifty yards from the house-house so the teacher-father and the father-teacher were omnipresent. Malcolm took to holding his breath. Wetting his bed. Dawdling on his way to and from collecting the billy of milk every morning from the Shepherds'. It was a sly form of torture that no one ever mentioned the stink of piss that haloed him, and when, at school, he got a whiff of the rabbiter's daughter, he knew they had something in common.

One morning-dawdle he saw a bird sitting in its nest, looking at him. Grey warblers weave hanging enclosed nests with feathers, moss, twigs, lichen, wool and dead leaves. They share parenting duties so Malcolm never knew if it was the mother or the father bird who poked its brownish-grey head out of the little hole in the side of the nest to stare at him inquisitively with eyes 'like frightened beads'. Above this window the grey warbler had made a miniature porch as a rain-shelter and it sat there, rain or shine, knitting worms and warming its eggs, minding its business. He saw it every morning and after a while when he got close the stay-at-home bird would hop out and let him put his finger in to count by feel how many eggs there were. It was warm and soft inside, a feather-lined orifice, and the two eggs seemed to glow under his finger. The parent-bird sat on a branch about a foot away eyeing Malcolm with a look of hysteria, and when he finished it would nip back. One day Malcolm put his finger in to check on the eggs and found there was an extra one, making it three. The new egg felt different, like the oval moon of an alien planet, and when he checked in Moncrieff's bird-book he discovered that the shining cuckoo is a parasitic bird that victimises the grey warbler by sneaking its own single egg in the side entrance of the hanging nest when the smaller bird is out gathering food, and in this way makes the grey warbler its substitute parent. The cunning cuckoo then

watches from a distance to see what the warbler will do, and for some unknown reason these maternal birds have never been known to reject a foreign egg. Because the cuckoo chick hatches earlier, the fledgling often ransacks the nest by tipping out any warbler chicks or eggs before it goes, leaving the doubly tricked bird doubly bereft. As an ally of the grey warbler Malcolm took against the cuckoo egg. It was a wrong egg, and he was glad it never hatched. But the discovery of this dramatic bird world was magic. When it rained the grey warbler's song got louder, as if the drops of water were tiny echo chambers. The Maori name for them is the onomatopoeic 'riro riro' and they sing with 'throatfuls of heartache'. After finding that first nest Malcolm discovered about six more in the area. He was still drawing incessantly, but drawing a bird or its nest couldn't show where it was and that was why, when he was about eight, he hit on the idea of mapping birds' nests.

Malcolm loves maps. They can tell you where you are when you're lost or at least give exact details of how to get to a place where you're unlikely to be found. The only paper he had was bread wrappers, the blank newsprint used in those days to wrap bread in, and he tried to keep the nest-map a secret from his prying parents, but they discovered it and began, hideously, like he knew they would, to encourage his bird-watching. To Malcolm, this encouragement was an invasion of his secret world and he bitterly resented it. His father's way of taking an interest was to clomp all over things and eggs were delicate. His mother seemed to have a physical aversion to Malcolm; he has no memory of her ever touching him, she was always typing. *Tap tap*, from the inside of the egg. Even his birth was Caesarian, that's why his beak is so perfect.

At this point I began to feel a little sorry for his ogre-parents who I'm sure thought they were doing the right thing in giving Malcolm's bird-watching their stamp of approval. Perhaps they didn't realise they were tormenting him? In those days hitting children was all the rage, an outlet for the disappointed. As if he sensed my sympathy straying and wanted to keep it company, Malcolm told me that throughout his childhood his mother read Jane Austen and Scottish, Irish, and Norwegian myths aloud to him and his brother. He related an incident where at about the age of nine, he wrote a story in the style of the myths and proudly showed it to her. She read it aloud

33

back to him, pronouncing phonetically all the incorrect words exactly as he'd written them, in a kind of dyslexic taunt.

Malcolm was quick to point out he was only a beginner at all this bird stuff; everybody knew more about it than him. The Shepherds' son Brian had a fantail he could lift off the eggs she was sitting on, then put back, like a lid he was opening and closing. Before Malcolm's family came, the Shepherds had been the only Pakeha and the Shepherd boys delighted in bullying the interlopers, putting them on the outer.

Malcolm also drew hills. Hills had personalities. Some were brooding, some friendly, some distant; one hill in particular was fearsome, another had a very long memory. It was a physiognomy of hills, portraits in silhouette, showing the bony knobs and humps and folds underneath the moth-eaten shawls of khaki. He drew them one at a time, never in groups, and always thought of hills as coming up from underneath. It was a long time before Malcolm realised that just as important was the wearing down or erosion of hills.

Motukiore Creek was an impoverished area. The pasture was nominal, gnawed-down bracken, and they were always walking barefoot on thorny gravel, like martyrs. Stone bruises and almost volcanic boils were endemic and Malcolm's mother helped out by taking music and doing first aid, lancing the infected stone bruises so the pus splattered out to the tune of 'Camptown Races', keeping time with the chime in her free hand. There was also a lot of lamenting. At school they learnt Maori laments and at home sang Scottish ones while doing the dishes:

Speed, bonnie boat, like a bird on the wing,
  Onward! the sailors cry;
Carry the lad that's born to be King
  Over the sea to Skye.
Loud the winds howl, loud the waves roar,
  Thunderclouds rend the air;
Mull was astern, Rum on the port,
  Eigg on the starboard bow.
Speed, bonnie boat, like a bird on a wing,
  Over the sea to Skye.

Malcolm's father was the only civil servant for miles and he automatically assumed all the other roles of government representative without inhibition, and also without ever, in his five years as teacher, policeman, welfare officer and health inspector, being admitted to any of the homes of the Maori – except once when somebody died and after being invited inside he ran out of the house at the sight of the dead body with its attendant widow. There was an unwritten rule in those days that Maori people did not admit Pakeha 'aristocrats' into their homes out of shame, and this arrangement was reciprocal. As kids Malcolm and his brother had immunity and had been inside almost every house. Except at the Tutares' place, where they stood on the roof in the feudal wind because there was no room inside.

Even while he himself was hitting Malcolm, his father was at the same time jailing local Maori for abusing their children. Malcolm finds this impossible to understand. Why did his mother let it happen? She was always looking elsewhere.

By some osmosis Malcolm had always known of his mother's intellectual past in Wellington, where she studied at the feet of scholars whose staggering footnotes were legendary. At about the same time as Malcolm began mapping the nests, a visiting party of these mythic academics descended on the house. They were Historic Places officials, mandarins in tweed, with polished vowels and pipes clenched between their teeth: J. C. Beaglehole OM, Professor Knight who was the government architect, Ormond Wilson, chairman of the Historic Places Trust and a member of the first Labour Government, and John Pascoe, National Archivist. They were so important that later, over the telephone, Malcolm wept as he gave me their exact titles, insisting I get absolutely correct every last syllable and detail of their honorifics. At dinner, he remembered, they started with corn on the cob and Ormond Wilson leaned across the table and loudly stage-whispered, 'Do we use our fingers?' When they departed in a whirl of tweed, a set of inch-to-a-mile 1943 topographical maps of the Hokianga slipped from their crevices and landed at Malcolm's feet. The maps were a revelation to him; from them he learnt about contour and scale and began to use estimated contours as a means of representing hills. He also discovered the use of symbols and keys on a map to represent such things as homes and bridges. One of the unstated bearings on Malcolm's nest-maps was for the homes of the various Maori boys he was in love with. Where they lived was richer terrain. But there was no symbol or key for them and even if there were, he would never have used it. These desirable boys were magnetic; they belonged to the landscape and Malcolm didn't. The nest-maps in some way linked him to them and I got the feeling it was no coincidence the grey warblers laid their eggs so close to the Maori boys. A map can be a kind of net. When the Puru brothers slid down the mud-bank into the creek they left ridges between their bum-marks that Malcolm found infinitely more interesting than birds or their nests – more like what he'd once felt for snapdragons.

Later, at Rangitane opposite the pa, he found a spring bubbling up from underneath the roots of a tree and had the breakthrough inspiration that this spring must have been the pa's water supply. In times of siege, access to it would have meant life or death.

His first notebook was made from bread wrappers and was $2\frac{1}{2}$ inches by $2\frac{1}{2}$ inches. He used that for times he went with the Shepherd boys when there were occasional lapses in their bullying. They loved killing things and were adept at it, capturing hawks in special gin traps and then whacking them on the head with fence battens to kill them. As a favour Malcolm was allowed to measure the wingspan of the dead hawks and to note the measurements in his miniature notebook in the tiny writing he had invented. Their forbidden pastime was foraging in the bush for food, looking for cabbage-tree shoots and the taraire berries that turn your teeth black. They walked with their heads down. If you saw a pile of owl shit and looked up there'd be a morepork sitting in a tree. They always use the same roost and because they are nocturnal, if you find one during the day it doesn't fly away. He thinks it was Brian Shepherd that first put him up to strangling a morepork. Brian said that by walking round and round the tree the morepork was roosting in you could persuade it to strangle itself. Once it spots you it glares at you with black-orbed golden eyes as big and vigilant as ticking clocks, every inch of the way. It can't take its eyes off you. So as you walk round the tree, at some point it has to whip its head around to keep you in sight or, so the theory went, continue until it wrings its own neck. The only problem was that, in order to walk in repeating circles, Malcolm had to occasionally look down to check his footing, so he never knew if the owl waited until he looked down to whip its head around or whether it was just about to strangle itself. No matter how many

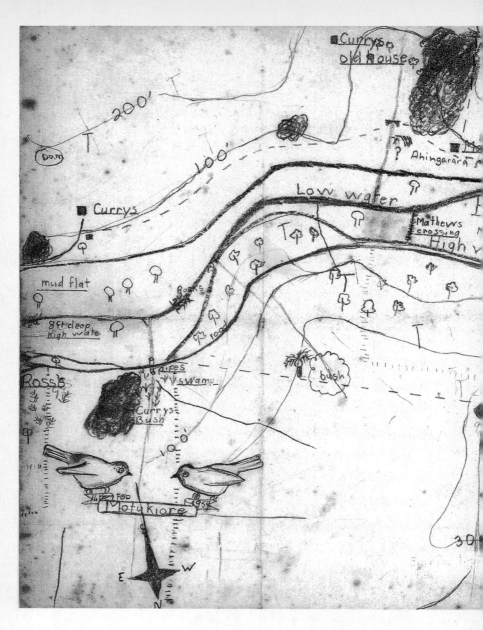

times he tried he never saw a morepork make that whipping movement or take its demonic, goat eyes off him. And he never managed to get one to strangle itself. Malcolm says he spent hours

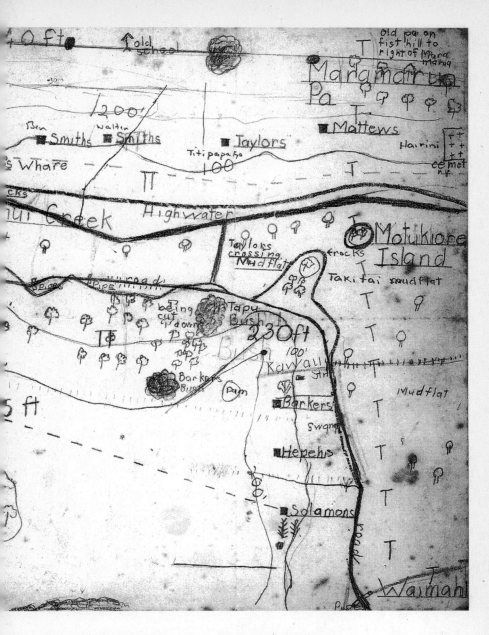

alone in the bush trying to solve this riddle.

At about the age of eleven, just before Malcolm went to boarding school, things went awry when his parents gave him an elementary bird-watching book. All the birds were laid out like anaesthetised patients on operating tables with their habits and measurements and characteristics carefully extracted and listed like a diagnosis. Even though Malcolm went on to join the Ornithological Society and became more sophisticated he felt the magic birdworld had slipped from his grasp.

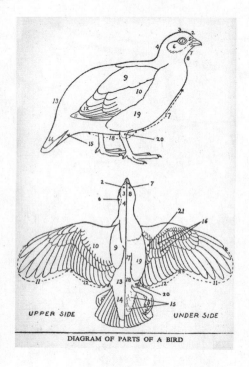

DIAGRAM OF PARTS OF A BIRD

1. Irides	12. Secondaries
2. Forehead	13. Rump
3. Crown	14. Upper Tail Coverts
4. Nape	15. Under Tail Coverts
5. Lores	16. Under Wing Coverts
6. Coverts	17. Breast
7. Chin	18. Belly
8. Throat	19. Flanks
9. Scapulars	20. Thighs
10. Upper Wing Coverts	21. Axillaries
11. Primaries	

Speculum = bar across wing of ducks

Malcolm still gets a thrill out of certain birds. He loves the accidental migrants such as the curlew and the red-tailed tropic bird or amakura, which is so rare he's never seen it. Also the white heron, the royal spoonbill and even the parasitic shining cuckoo, which spends the New Zealand winter in Indonesia and then, after five months, flies back to the same area which contains the grey warblers in whose nest it previously left its egg. The journey back is so long the cuckoo reputedly carries a tiny pebble in its claws to lick to assuage the pangs of a terrible thirst. Malcolm recently saw a fernbird when the bus to Whangarei broke down and made an unscheduled stop in the middle of nowhere. Out of habit he recorded the sighting on his bus-ticket in tiny bird-writing. Malcolm says that seeing an old hawk is very unusual; you can determine their age by the fact that as they grow older they go silver, just like people. He has, once or twice, even seen hawks in cities. Somehow they have drifted off course. These lost hawks, to him, represent isolation.

During our talk, Leo, who usually avoids Malcolm because of the smell of cigarettes, moved closer to his chair, using that insinuating, twining movement cats have perfected. He seemed to be following the story closely but when Malcolm reached the listed menu of birds he turned his back and stalked off in a huff.

The image of Malcolm walking round and round a tree with his eyes locked in combat with the glaring owl haunted me, and as I listened to what he said, another part of me was busy remembering a time when I too first came face to face with something that has never since taken its eyes off me.

– 4 –

The birthday of the world

At the end of 1989 I was living in Wellington, the tremulous capital of New Zealand, quietly pursuing my dreams of total world domination. While rehearsing *Passion Play*, a new work, with my long-time colleague and otherworldly muse Kilda, I began to notice

that my body, which was strong from years of dancing, seemed to be taking longer and longer to recover. After a hard day and an alcohol-soaked sleep I was accustomed to bouncing back, like a coiled spring. But now each day it felt as if my strength was being slowly drained away. My limbs seemed gloved in lead. My whole body was like an obedient working dog that, for some reason it was powerless to communicate, could carry out its usual duties only with the greatest

difficulty. For as long as possible I shook off these warning signals and found that with an exaggerated, almost fascist determination

I could still perform even the most punishing movements. But increasingly I felt like Superman accidentally (perhaps deliberately?) exposed to the one thing that could destroy him, kryptonite, and time was running out. We went ahead with our performances as planned and on the last night we were nearing the end of the hour-long duet when the entire room lurched to the side, upending me into a dizzying darkness then hurling me onto what I thought was a wall. As I attempted to recover I noticed that Kilda and the other occupants of the room, the audience, had not been affected by this earthquake. As Kilda gathered me into her arms to guide me through the last section I was dimly grateful that the work we were perform-ing was one in which sudden collapses to the floor and agonised pietas were not out of place. The only prop was a monumental arm, cast in ice, hanging in the corner, its index finger pointing into a tin bucket. That night it seemed like the frigid hand of God had found its guilty target and was sending me down, a drop at a time. After the performance the beer I loved tasted like frog's piss and even the compliments I craved couldn't keep me from crawling home to bed.

The next morning my left ear and the left side of my head hurt, as if someone were blowing up an angry little balloon inside my head with an evil message written on it, and the whole world seemed to be on a slight tilt. In the following days the last dregs of marrow were sucked from my bones. *Passion Play* was booked to open in London the following month and I kept putting off the decision to cancel, certain this was a minor and temporary setback. Then one morning I discovered I no longer had the strength to walk the fifty metres to the shop after setting out, determined to succeed, only to find I had to stop halfway, panting, holding onto the handrail, my legs crumbling beneath me. At that moment I realised the question was

44

not whether I could get to London, or even the shop, but whether I could get back.

I was living in Roseneath in a two-bedroomed flat in a large concrete Art Deco building precariously perched on a cliff overlooking the sea. Although there must have been another person living there I only ever remember being alone, or being visited. In the minutes, hours, days and weeks that followed, I went from doctor to naturopath, to ear specialist to faith-healer, then back to the doctor, searching for a name I could attach to my condition. Before I became more or less bed-ridden, when I walked down the street the people I passed seemed to emit a screeching static, as if they were clawing their fingernails down a blackboard inside me. The sensation was almost unbearable and my raids in quest of a diagnosis became increasingly panicked.

In between this searching I spent what felt like years in the living-room, at the window gazing out to sea. Every morning two plucky red tug-boats breasted the waves going from left to right across my window, off to a day's work tugging, and every evening, just before dark, they came back. One was slightly bigger than the other and was always just ahead while the distance between them was precisely the same. They were old boats, faithful to each other, somehow Scandinavian and with their cheerful red colour against the blue, white-frothed waves I felt in some obscure way they knew I was watching and, by dint of being punctual, were trying to comfort me. I also loved to watch the inter-island ferry as it slowly moved, much further out than the tug-boats, towards the last finger of land before disappearing behind it into Cook Strait and on to the South Island. From my point of view the ferry looked as if it was heading straight towards the land and its slow eating up of the distance between them filled me with an ecstasy of anticipation and longing. Each time I witnessed this event a part of me was convinced the ferry would somehow, in its inexorable way, begin to push back the headland or be crushed by it and when the last millimetre of space remained it was as if a miraculous disaster was about to occur. The fact that the boat always disappeared behind the finger of land did not disappoint me. In the complete silence of its vanishing it looked to me as if it had sailed straight into its opponent and, finding no noticeable resistance, was now, out of sight, tunnelling serenely underground.

When I finally received the diagnosis that was in those days regarded as an automatic death sentence, my reaction was strange, even to myself. That first afternoon I shed a few cold tears and then sat with some shell-shocked friends as they fumbled for the appropriate phrase. I felt sorry for them. They were like actors who had forgotten their lines, trying clumsily to help each other fill the greedy silence. And it was my job to let them know they hadn't failed. This I tried to do as best I could, in the same fumbling way. Malcolm called me from a telephone box in Auckland for the news and we had a wooden conversation. Then, after more of the same, I fell into a deep, dreamless sleep. When I came to it was morning and I felt as if an immense weight had been lifted from me. As I was doing the dishes in the poky little kitchen I was filled with a wild joy. The inane words 'this is the birthday of the world, this is the birthday of the world' kept singing in my head.

The lightness I felt then reminds me of the feeling of weight-lessness I used to experience in that childhood game where you stand in a doorway and press your arms as hard as you can for as long as you can against the door frame. Then when you feel you can't stand it any more, you quickly step out of the frame, relax your arms and marvel as, of their own free will, they begin to float up. Except on that morning, it wasn't just my arms that were helium-filled, but all of me; as if I had somehow, without knowing it, been pushing with all my might against an invisible structure exactly my shape for years and years, if not forever, and now, with the uttering of a few words the crushing frame had been magically removed or dissolved, releasing me into the ether. And if it were spoken words that released me, it stands to reason that it must have been spoken words that created this prison in the first place, and what they were and how they got there still causes me to wonder.

I sometimes think the feeling of relief came with the unconscious knowledge that I no longer had to destroy myself, the virus would do it for me. That day the desire to drink alcohol left me and has never come back.

Whatever the cause, my newborn lightness and helplessness floated me into a world seething with helpers. In an atmosphere comparable to a kind of amniotic fluid this alternative world was a place where irrevocably wounded people were lovingly guided in their search for the one thing that would cure them. The ancient idea of a quest brings immediately to mind a person, young or old, male or female, fat or thin, setting out, usually alone, on a road to some- where. But in my case it felt more as if I was not moving at all; I was sitting or more often lying while a succession of healers, each burning with news about the one true cure only they possessed, came up to me and for a small fee did their bit. I was told to put away my coffin, to cancel my funeral plans, and to drink this juice squeezed from the bark of a sacred tree; to stare softly at colours; to sniff gently at smells; to not wash at all for three weeks and lie at four o'clock in the morning on the night of the full moon in the freezing

I like myself the way I am.
I love myself the way I am.

I am a gorgeous open and healthy
being who is lovingly living a
creative and honest life.
The child of my being is totally
accepted and unconditionally loved.
I therefore have fun in my maturity
As my happiness shines within and
to all around. I am content.

I am very assertive and keenly
sensitive to my own needs with an
awareness to the needs of others
I am strong. I lovingly accept myself
So I can openly express how I feel

I am a kind and compassionate
being.

I am a light being who is
unconditionally loved and who loves
without attachment. I am honest
with myself and truthful to others
For I am a light being.

I am a beautiful beautiful being
I am compassionate and caring loving and gentle
I love unconditionally and I am deeply and
profoundly loved by the love of my life
and all those around me.

Divine light is flowing through my
being radiating Empathy, Honesty Serenity
and calmness to every cell of my being
and to the world all around.

With each breath I energize and nourish
every cell of my being
I live in gods light, I see gods
light in all things.

☺ I am a calm and loving being
At peace with myself and the
Universe. From my pool of calmness
I express myself and feelings clearly
and with sensitivity.
I am a calm and loving being.

☺ I am a wonderful being who is
kind and considerate, gentle, forgiving
and nurturing. I give of myself freely
and am open to recieve the divine
abundance of the universe
I am at peace and unafraid for I
am greatly greatly loved.
Indeed Indeed Indeed.

As I feel the joy of my being flowing
with its light and love. As I feel
inspiration and creativity unfolding, so do
I feel the joy and peace of being in
☺ harmony with the universe — myself

I am a being of light filled with
the inspiration, independence, worth, creativity
and laughter of creation I am glowing with life

I am an open, affectionate, warm, successful
☺ and creative woman (man) who gets on
well with people. I am fit and healthy
All is comfortable in my world.

I am a happy gay person, content with
my high standards that I easily maintain
I am glowingly healthy, ingenious and interesting
I am a caring, compassionate and loving being
I am myself

I am a gorgeous open and healthy
being who is lovingly living a creative and
honest life. In my maturity my happiness
☺ shines within and to all around
I am content.

48

water at Takapuna beach while a yawning healer said prayers over me; to imagine my father as a pile of old newspapers then beat him to death with a black rubber hose; to have my aura cleansed with crystals; to listen to channelled aliens and thousand-year-old entities making lame jokes about my past lives; to drink my own urine; eat no meat, wheat, or sugar; to feel no blame, speak my truth, but above all, without delay, to love myself. If only, I was told, I could completely and utterly accept and love myself I would immediately be flooded with light and healed. One audio-tape shared around a rapidly diminishing inner circle of fellow searchers began in an American-accented woman's voice, 'I love you. I really love you.' Following detailed instructions I stared at myself in a mirror and tried in all sincerity to tell my reflection that I loved it, or you, or me. It was all so confusing and embarrassing I finally had to admit defeat. I could not love myself enough so I deserved to die.

There was however a slender ray of hope. My naturopath Peter suggested I learn to meditate. He explained the simplest method to me and every day I sat for about twenty minutes and, with no noticeable results, tried to do it. Then when a little of my energy had returned he told me about an intensive ten-day meditation course in the South Island that was about to begin. It sounded gruelling, but I had tried everything else so I signed up.

49

– 5 –

Volcano

On the application form and in the brochure for the Buddhist meditation retreat there was a long list of rules with one rule that intrigued me. I could understand the no eating meat, no sex, no smoking, no talking, no drinking or drug-taking, no bad language, no touching, no stealing, no wearing of lewd or improper clothing, but the rule *no sleeping in high and luxurious beds* caught my attention. The phrase impressed me. It led me to wonder what experiences could be had in high and luxurious beds that were not available in low, less opulent ones. Presumably the height and luxury of any bed could not in itself cause its occupant to sin? Or perhaps the writer of these rules had experienced or seen at first hand evidence of the corrupting influence of height and comfort? Would there possibly be the odd high and luxurious bed strewn about the place for us to resist? Or, as I pondered the problem further, was the inclusion of such a provocative rule a covert signal to lovers of comfort that they should go elsewhere, or at least on arrival at the course, surrender all such beds they had somehow managed to smuggle in? Then I began to worry exactly what kind of bed I'd be required to sleep in and hurried to fill in full details of my medical condition in the tiny gap next to the words 'special needs' in the hope an exception might be made for me if we were required to sleep on the floor.

All this worrying made me think of Nana Wright, my father's long-dead mother who was a dedicated, even passionate worrier. She and my mother often sat in Nana's smoke-stained front room with the picture of Jesus proferring his flaming heart over the fireplace, worrying together. For some reason I was often there too, sitting at the table a little off to the side, watching and listening. Though I have long since forgotten any specific concern, what lingers in memory is the quality of their voices rising and falling in the darkened room; the vowels of commiseration like the sounds a mother cat makes when she is calling for her blind, groping litter. They worried about each other, about their husbands, sons, fathers and daughters and even their own mothers. But it was the men in our family who needed the most worrying. The men in our family drank, had always drunk, and continue to drink. And their drinking caused them to do things that were hurtful to their wives, children and mothers, things they regretted. Things I see now that worried them so much, they drank to forget.

But there was another reason for me to think of Nana Wright as I was filling out the application form for the meditation retreat. Religion. Buddhism was a religion and my only previous contact with religion had been through her. Nana Wright had been a devout Catholic and for several years when I was a child she used to take me to Sunday morning Mass at the Catholic church on River Road in Tuakau where we lived. Very early on these mornings I would dress in shorts and a white shirt and tie in front of the fireplace. With the outstretched heart of Jesus flaming above us, Nana, standing slightly behind me, would knot my tie with her gnarled, walnut fingers. I can still feel her whispered breath in my ear as she surreptitiously slipped a coin into my shirt pocket 'for the collection plate'. I loved going to church. God lived there. The priest wore a long purple dress and spoke in a strange language whose meaning hovered like a bird, just out of reach. There was incense, holy water, life-size statues of Jesus and Mary with crowns on and stained-glass windows that made the light float down in magical beams of colour. When we entered, before we sat in the pew, Nana crossed herself and did a tiny curtsy. Everything was clean and strict, with special names. For years my most fervent wish was to be a priest, to wear the dress and speak the language. I remember being Confirmed, an affirmation I longed for, by a visiting Bishop so august that, to me at least, he was almost invisible. A ghostly finger, dipped in oil, reached out of a cloud and touched me on the forehead, between my eyebrows. After that I was allowed to receive Holy Communion every Sunday, kneeling with the grown-ups, our mouths gaping open like a frozen choir for the priest to put the round, white wafer in. It was the body of Christ and Nana nudged me, whispering, 'Don't chew!' And we had to go to Confession, to confess our sins. I knew what a sin was. And I also automatically knew that what I really did wrong and what I really thought wrong was so monstrous I couldn't possibly feed it through the bars to the invisible, breathing presence waiting on the other side. So I spent all week making up sins I thought a boy my age, size and build would be most likely to commit. And then, as if in reply, they banned the strange language I loved so much and Mass was said in English. Gradually I forgot I ever wanted to be a priest.

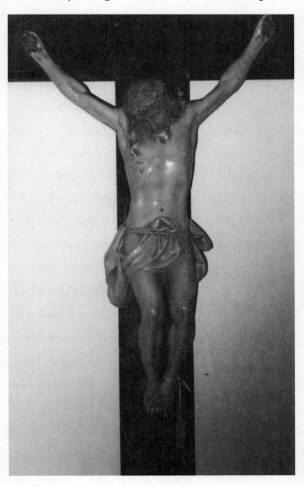

But the Buddhists never mentioned God and they had their own word for sin. It was just that the phrase *high and luxurious beds* reminded me of the part of me that had been forbidden, by myself, on behalf of Him.

The meditation course was held about an hour's drive out of Christchurch. I was met at the airport by an organiser and then, along with the teacher, a fiercely anonymous middle-aged Asian woman who was also waiting there, was driven deep into the Canterbury Plains. We arrived in the lengthening shadows of late afternoon. The course was held in a series of low, spartan buildings usually used by Boy Scouts. One largish block contained a kitchen and eating area, some bedrooms with bunks (high but not luxurious), and communal showers and toilet-stalls. Another building had a meditation room with an air of high expectation, and more sleeping areas. In between these two blocks, on a slight incline there was a small one-room structure that reminded me of the dental clinic at school, what we called the 'murder house'. This room was for the teacher. These buildings were grouped around an informal court-yard, with a hill extending up behind the teacher's house. There seemed to be no other buildings for miles, just the wind and sun-burnished plains, poplars marching in straight lines into the distance and an infinite acreage of sky. As we went in I noticed a couple of people busily sectioning off different areas of the outside space with lengths of string attached to prongs stuck into the ground, like those waist-high electric fences to keep cattle in. I soon discovered the fences were being erected to segregate the sexes, for the entire length of the course, to avoid distraction. The bleat, 'But what if you're gay?' died on my lips. After a light meal and a brief meeting in which the gruelling timetable and various additional rules (no staring, no distracting gestures) were explained, we entered a silence that could only be broken, we were told, in an emergency.

Later that evening, under an immense sky blazing with stars, I gathered with the other male students outside the door of the meditation room and, old students first, one by one we were gently ushered in.

The course was directed, in his absence, by the pre-recorded voice of the founder of the Vipassana Foundation, a Mr Goenka. The teacher, who sat on a slightly raised platform at the head of the room, controlled a tape machine that she turned on and off. The rich deep voice that came out of this machine said many things. There were detailed instructions in the meditation technique, warnings of possible pitfalls, exhortations to be strong, to never give up, and a persuasive, eloquent explication of the causes of human suffering and its remedy. Mr Goenka told us that, according to the Buddha, we suffer because we crave and cling to whatever we desire, and try to push away that which we dislike. Our minds are like chattering monkeys, either raking over past glories and insults, or worrying about our illustrious futures and plotting revenge on those who had wronged us; rarely, if ever, resting in peaceful awareness in the present moment. 'Don't take my word for it,' Mr Goenka said. 'See for yourself!' And, he went on, because the nature of physical existence is change, all is impermanence, everything dies, so we are destined to suffer loss again and again. But as Mr Goenka explained, there is a Way to escape this cycle of craving and aversion, a Way called the Dharma which the Buddha unveiled for humankind, in his wisdom and compassion. The Dharma is embodied in The Eightfold Noble Path, eight seemingly simple rules for living, and in practising an ancient meditation technique we were extremely lucky to now be in a position to receive. It was a priceless opportunity indeed, Mr Goenka stressed, requiring possibly thousands of lifetimes of overcoming bad karma, to even be in this room at this moment, being offered this gift. Take refuge in the Buddha and the Dharma, he urged. Strive for Enlightenment!

The meditation technique involved a laborious process in which we sharpened then focused our sharpened minds on the nearest thing at hand, our own bodies. For example, if you close your eyes and concentrate on, say, the left side of your skull, after a while you can feel the sensations that live there, the 'skullnesses', and simply observe them. At first the voice guided us. Systematically, eyes closed, inch by screaming inch we, or rather our minds, crawled like pilgrims over the vast topography of a country whose tempestuous history was locked deep within. We were strongly advised not to judge the sensations we encountered in this journey, just to observe them calmly, and then calmly move on to the next designated area. In order to perform this process, Mr Goenka explained, it was imperative we sit, for sessions lasting an hour at a time, cross-legged on our cushions, backs straight, completely still. The day, which began at 4 a.m. and ended at 9.30 p.m., was divided into nine or ten of these sessions, with short breaks in between. At first we were permitted to move slightly, if our discomfort was too great, or even to stand by our cushions for a short time, still meditating. In severe cases that might lead to movements or sounds that would distract others, one was reluctantly allowed to leave the room for a short walk. While most of the old students were famously still, the back rows of beginners that I was in were seething with an involuntary discontent. One morning someone began to snicker, then to giggle helplessly as if at a joke they were desperately trying to forget. Then, around the room, barks of unsuccessfully stifled laughter showed that the joke had somehow spread. When there were about five people in the throes of guttural convulsions so irresistible I was about to join in, the teacher's voice rang out, 'Would those people who are laughing please leave the room now.' And they gratefully did. During the entire hilarious episode, all the participants, to the best of my knowledge, had their eyes closed.

Sometimes the room was a forest of agitated rustling, punctuated by deep sighs of boredom or despair. One person, after repeatedly leaving the room, was never seen or heard again. It was as if each time he walked out he went a little further away, until finally he was ejected so far, by the force of his ungovernable emotions, there was no coming back. In some ways this person's audible struggle was akin to the struggle I was experiencing trying to prevent my mind from straying. Just when it was finally focused on the object of its concentration it would sneakily, like a person who is massaging you with one hand while talking on the telephone with the other, find a way to cheat. Bringing it back, without anger, time and time again, was a task I found fiendishly difficult. But I was determined to persevere. It was tempting, at times, to surreptitiously punish the body I was trying, in this drastic way, to free. But Mr Goenka's voice urged the Middle Way, the way of patience, equanimity and mindfulness, and I was beginning to trust his voice. So far, everything he had said tallied with my experience.

Sometimes he chanted in Sanskrit; a language, like Latin, reputedly dead. But the words he used were so living, so succulent, I felt he was feeding me, a morsel at a time through the bars of the cage I was trapped in, an essential food. One day I discovered I could feel the voice vibrating in my body and could use it, as if it were singing directly to the area I was working on. Then it was as if each section of flesh was a document tattooed in Braille and the voice was chanting the text aloud, erasing it as it went.

At other times I thought I was going mad, that we were all mad;

57

bodies without a voice following the instructions of a voice without a body. One morning someone walked out of the meditation room and could be heard in the distance for what seemed like hours sobbing, screaming, howling and keening in an inconsolable grief.

As the course progressed, when I was sitting in the meditation room with my eyes closed, I began to recognise many of my fellow participants by the sounds they made. Everyone had their own signature music of walking in, sitting down and getting up, even of breathing. Similarly, during breaks and meals, because we could not speak, our bodies seemed to helplessly express what our words would have concealed. The act of putting down a spoon, or picking one up, somehow managed to convey, by subtle changes in emphasis and timing, an endless variety of meanings ranging from profound joy to bitter contempt.

At first excessive politeness reigned. If two people arrived at the table of food at the same time, the usual, 'No, you go first,' 'No you,' exchange became, robbed of the simple words that would solve it, a microscopic duel of stops and starts and respectfully muted gestures until an agreement was reached. If someone sat down directly opposite me, the meal became, for me at least, a battle of wits. To catch someone looking at you or, worse, to be caught, felt to me in those first days like a criminal offence. I solved this by keeping my eyes averted, only to discover as the course progressed that when I summoned the courage to look up there were all sorts of gazes roaming around, basking and feeding like peaceful animals in the sun. We were creatures of habit. Always sitting in the same spot on the hillside, strolling the same stroll, liking to be near or wanting to avoid the same people. The one person who for no logical reason I took a dislike to seemed, at times, to multiply himself. On days when

I was irritable he would be there, in my face, at every turn, as if he were a spy hired to test my equanimity. The people around me reminded me of characters in a myth. Somehow I knew that the dark, hurried boy who was always crossing my path was a Renaissance prince in exile, another man was an old woman – a stepmother – another a donkey, yet another a kind of flurried duck; one was primarily an uncle, another a distant cousin, a pretender to the throne . . .

In the evenings, after the day's work, we sat in relaxed positions in the meditation room and watched videos of Mr Goenka. He told us pithy stories from the life of Gautama, the Buddha, in such a witty, mischievous way that we laughed like tickled children. I remember in one story when somebody tripped over somebody in the street Mr Goenka, taking on the voice of the injured party, kept repeating the words, 'Have you got eyes or buttonholes, eyes or buttonholes?' in tones of mock outrage. When we were helplessly laughing he nimbly thrust the moral of the story, like a knife, right in, and sat back like a golden frog on his lily pad, beaming at us. In one of these videos his wife sat silently beside him, an elderly, dignified Indian woman in a sari. They were sitting on a high platform, cross-legged, like statues, and her sari overflowed the edge of the platform like a waterfall suspended in exquisite folds. Even her spectacles seemed eternal, carved in stone.

In the last few days the pressure was increased. Now, every afternoon, we had one hour-long session in which we were asked to remain completely still for the entire period, to not move an inch. As we prepared for these sittings, extreme precautions had to be taken. Tiny tucks in a cushion, bunched-up seams of under-wear, ticklish fringes of shawls, all these slight, at first almost imperceptible, discomforts had to be attended to. If not they grew, over the course of the hour, into sensations so annoying, even painful, that to refrain from making the slight movement that would correct them was torture. Gradually I discovered that no matter how long I spent arranging myself there was always some detail that escaped my attention; sometimes even the rearranging itself was at fault, until I came to understand this was an intrinsic discomfort. The periods of meditation were started and finished by the sound of a bell. If my concentration was sustained the bell tolled victory. If my mind, more often than not, wandered, the bell that would end the session was like the distant sight of water, perhaps a mirage, to a man drowning in sand.

Now I had a map, the painstaking journey over my body was becoming more familiar and increasingly I was able to observe the sensations I encountered without either craving them if they were pleasant, or trying to push them away if they were not. I began to see images flashing, images of things that had happened to me, things I had done, things I hadn't thought of in years. They were like brief out-takes from a well-known film; short segments that never made it into the official version. These potent fragments seemed to be buried in the exact part of my body where they had been most felt, trapped there by the force of my original reaction, and it was only now by the focused beam of an impartial concentration that they could be projected and seen again. In one flickering clip I saw an old man riding a bicycle and as he rode a trail of pound notes flew out of his pocket and onto the street. And I saw myself as a little boy running after him picking up the notes like a hen pecking up a line of grain, in the firm belief that now I was rich. Then I saw my mother taking me by the hand to the old man's crooked house to give him back his money. This was all speeded up, conveyed in a flash. There were many more magic-lantern flashes like this but what they lit up has now gone again.

We were told that if we felt it was necessary we could stay focused on a particular part of our bodies for a little longer than usual. Soon after this caveat I was working on my chest when I felt a curious bulging, something welling up, so I went over the area again with my fine-toothed mind combing it very slowly and carefully. Then it was as if my chest was an orifice and I struggled to remain impartial as it excreted what felt like bucketfuls of thick, black tar that I knew was the essence of grief. It was an indescribable relief and went on and on as I played the role of witness. This was no hazy, suggestive feeling, it was as real as shitting and afterwards, under the spangled sky, my chest felt newborn, as light as a feather on a breath.

One evening, while I was working on my left forearm, I began to feel another sensation not mentioned in the list of warnings and rules or in any of Mr Goenka's talks; a sensation that, as it grew, turned into something no warning or rule could ever contain. Initially a sexual arousal, it didn't stop at my genitals but began, unbelievably, to creep higher. If I paid any attention to it, this powerful in-rising stopped or withdrew a little, back into its cave, but when I used all my strength to ignore it and continued working on my arm, it slithered like a fat, juicy snake up the marrow of my spine. What happened next was inconceivable. It would be an understatement to compare it with a thousand orgasms, a thousand rushes of heroin, even years of continual praise experienced simultaneously in one body over the course of approximately 30 seconds. The duration of the event is, in any case, almost impossible to gauge. It was as if my spine was a sexual organ, ejaculating in gushes of blinding light out

61

of the top of my head. I felt the way a volcano must feel when, after centuries of lying dormant, it finally blows its stack. When the eruption was over, although 'over' is not quite the right word as I can still feel the ripples, I opened my eyes to see if the walls or the people around me were splattered with holy come. But despite my state of extreme ecstasy, nothing else had changed. Unable to contain myself, at the end of the session when the teacher was available for private questions I explained my experience to her and humbly asked for advice. A part of me thought I had just been enlightened and was about to be proclaimed as a Buddha. But she said such experiences were not uncommon on the Path and were possible traps. One must take care not to be caught up in them.

In the break after this session, as we stood in a loose group looking up at the night sky with its rash of stars, one of the stars began, undeniably, to move. There was a low murmur as we all noticed it at once. Then as we all watched, the distant point of light moved again. The desire to speak was intense, and as it passed there was a feeling of joy, almost celebration, at allowing something to retain its mystery.

Despite the teacher's words, over the last few days of the course I shamefully tried to get the ecstatic event to happen again. I could feel the snake, as I thought of it, coiled, chthonic, tantalisingly near. I tried luring it, ignoring it, coaxing, begging, even commanding it but all my efforts seemed to drive it away. It seemed to know me better than I did. Even though I could get the snake to begin its ascent, now I had tasted the Bliss, there was no way I could completely ignore it. Like something feral that instinctively knows if it comes close enough to take the bait it will be captured, the serpent always retreated back into the depths when my mind so much as glanced its way.

Then I realised this was the most difficult test. Though I had been able in some ways to keep my equilibrium when in pain and discomfort, I couldn't imagine ever not wanting Bliss.

Mr Goenka had been promising us a treat, a healing balm for the wounds of our incisions and on the last day we were given the last gift. This was the practice of loving-kindness. One began by thinking of a person one loved and allowing the feelings to flow towards them like mother's milk, then gradually extending this loving feeling to others we knew. Then came the hard bit: we were urged to put someone we disliked in place of the loved one and keep the milk of loving-kindness flowing towards our enemies. Here my teats almost dried up and I had to quickly sneak back someone more acceptable to keep flowing. But I found after several attempts there were people I managed to forgive for wrongs long cherished. Then we were given a prayer which was a plea for all sentient beings to be happy, to be purified of their defilements, to be liberated from suffering, and after we prayed for the entire universe and everything that breathed, we were asked to send the milk of loving-kindness to ourselves.

After the course, back in Wellington, I was brimful of something so unfamiliar it took me a while to comprehend. As I began planning my next dance work, *Gloria*, I realised that after years of discontent, I was simply grateful to be alive and wanted to give thanks.

5 foot 8

During the mid to late 1980s I had been living and working in New York as a dancer in the Paul Taylor Company which regularly toured both America and Europe. Sometimes, after these tours, I had a short break before the next rehearsals began. Through Tobias, a writer and explorer in his sixties who doted on me, I met a circle of writers, painters and intellectuals of my grandparents' generation. One summer I ended up in Italy for a week or two and decided to spend time in Rome and Florence, sightseeing and visiting museums. Tobias had given me the number of Ugo, an Italian friend of his who lived in Rome, and one afternoon I met him for the first and only time for a drink in a bar at the foot of the Spanish Steps. I don't remember much of our conversation. Nervous of his obvious sophistication and anxious to impress, I probably prattled on about all the art I'd seen, and the proximity of the death-place of Keats. Ugo was a big man, in his late forties or early fifties, with thatched eyebrows and a tremendous moustache that reminded me of one of those topiary bushes clipped and re-clipped until they resemble and are made to continue resembling giant animals. And in the same way as these leafy animals come to life in the wind, as he talked Ugo's moustache gently flapped its wings. Under their hairy awning, his eyes twinkled as he laughed and talked and drank me in. At the end of our brief meeting, as he was leaving, Ugo warned me to be on the lookout for something he called the Stendhal syndrome. This syndrome, he explained, was a rare condition only found in spinsters or ex-schoolteachers from the Antipodes. Such people, he said, who had never been to Europe in their lives and in the most severe cases had never before been out of the country of their birth, were sometimes found at the end of the day wandering in public places in Rome and in Florence, so overcome by all the magnificent art they'd crammed in during a single day that they didn't know where they were and couldn't even remember their own names. Sometimes, he quipped, they were even found mooing like cows or baaing like sheep. We both laughed at this good joke but I remember as I laughed feeling a slight spasm of fear.

In Florence, in the middle of an art-crammed day, after admiring and walking around Michelangelo's *David*, I sat down to rest in a corner of the Academy. From there I could still see the statue, under its glass cupola, and was also perfectly placed to watch the other tourists as they came into the room. As they rounded the corner in droves, in the few seconds before they caught sight of David they pre-arranged their faces into expressions of awe or indifference, almost as if they were there not to see the sculpture, but to be seen by it. I heard low murmurs of, 'There he is,' and a volley of indrawn breaths. And then it was as if the already ecstatic expressions had nowhere left to go. The actual encounter was an anticlimax and needed to be clipped and re-clipped by the parasitic snapping of cameras so that it could be made to fit into the cut-out shape of some long-lost original encounter. Some people smiled fiercely to avoid betraying their unworthiness, but most set to work with the cameras and superlatives. Although watching this phenomenon made me feel superior, I couldn't help recognising that my own experience had, minus the camera, been exactly the same.

In my solitary wanderings through art galleries and museums I always avoided those large groups, usually Japanese, German, or American, that move from famous painting to famous painting like swarms of insects, each guided by an expert. The sight of such groups with their cameras, and the postcards, posters and catalogues we were encouraged, for a small price, to carry away, made me realise

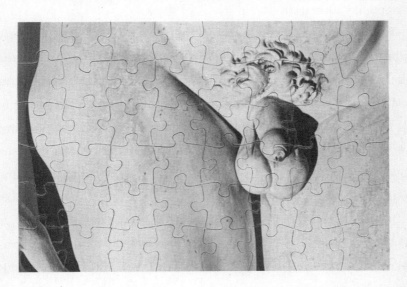

that the endless reproduction of a thing is somehow, in inverse increments, also the history of its death.

There are famous works of art that have escaped. One winter, in Vienna, after checking in to our hotel, a group of us jet-lagged dancers decided to visit the Kunsthistorisches Museum as a way of trying to stay awake. The city was infested with black crows the size of small children and they watched us intently as we trudged through the snow past a pair of German shepherds at each other's throats until we arrived, surprisingly unharmed, at the Museum. Once inside we wandered like sleepwalkers through the giant, deserted building, eventually ending up fast asleep on a circular banquette where we were supposedly sitting to look more closely at a roomful of vicious German crucifixions. Before I succumbed, I remember walking slowly past a series of portraits of old people by Rembrandt. The people in these paintings gazed back at me, through the accumulated shadows of three hundred years, as surprised as I was to find themselves still alive, in a kind of suspended animation.

Whenever I had been away on tour and was driving back into Manhattan from the airport, the first glimpse of the city through the girders of the Brooklyn Bridge was breath-taking. Just before it was visible there were miles of graveyards, rank on rank of grey tombstones, and as the skyscrapers leapt into view, for an instant it was always as if the tombstones were the stunted children of these towering monuments. I felt both lucky and frightened to live in one of them.

It's a curious coincidence that today, the day I'm writing this, is September the 11th 2002, the first anniversary of the infamous terrorist attacks on New York City. When I turned on the radio this morning the opening outcry of Mozart's 'Requiem', being sung here live in memory of the dead, overcame me like the first crashing breakers of an ocean of grief that had taken a whole year to finally reach me.

Beginning in late 1983, I was living in a technically illegal sub-let in a project building on the Lower Eastside. My bedroom was literally on the sharp edge of the building's precipice. I slept right on the corner, seven storeys up, with my head on 1st Avenue, my body parallel with 3rd Street and my feet pointing to the East River. At night the sound of traffic was like the sound of my own blood swishing through my veins, sirens wailing. As I lay there I often thought of the person lying a few feet above me, the one just beneath me and all the others above, below and beside me, and I imagined all the buildings and furniture gone revealing us floating in space, each in our own plot of thin air, in rows and rows and rows, travelling through dreams and nightmares.

My room-mate was Brian Carbee, a Bostonian who had danced with me in the Limbs Dance Company in New Zealand. We met him when the Company was at the American Dance Festival in North Carolina in 1981. I saw Brian dancing at a party there and was so impressed with his boogying I went up and made friends. He liked us and we liked him so he came back to dance in New Zealand. I remember standing with Brian in downtown Auckland the day he arrived, feeling embarrassed at this poor excuse for a city. We were never lovers, more like brothers with a shared taste in black men, and now he had come to New York. He was cute, a kind of futuristic frontiersman with a cartoon face, a jaw of granite and a zany sense of humour.

When Limbs stayed on a marae in Rotorua for a weekend of

69

sharing, there was a tohunga or traditional priest who took a liking to Brian and me. His name was Irirangi, which means 'voice of the spirits'. He praised the colour of my aura and knew things about me he shouldn't. We all slept together in the meeting-house and on the last day Irirangi made a speech in which he named Brian and me after the neighbouring volcanoes because, like them, he said, we were 'white on top'. I was Tongariro and Brian was Ruapehu. I remember a slight feeling of embarrassment, as if the names were too big for us, followed quickly by a twinge of disappointment that Brian's mountain was taller. Then Irirangi asked me to step forward and stand completely still in front of him while he performed a frightening dance with a wooden patu, swirling and cutting the air around my head with a flurry of nimble slashes and jabbing movements, pulling faces and sticking his tongue out at me. I must have passed the test because he gave me the carved patu and I took it to New York as my good-luck charm. There was something fishy about Irirangi; if I asked other Maori people about him they fell silent and, years later when I heard he had died, nobody would elaborate. He died of throat cancer or by choking on a fish-bone, I can't remember which; I just remember thinking the voice of the spirits had been silenced and wondering if he'd said something he shouldn't. But I liked him. And now Douglas Tongariro and Brian Ruapehu were on a different summit. It must have been difficult for Brian living with me because we were at opposite ends of the dance food-chain. Like most dancers in Manhattan Brian worked as a waiter and lived in hope of getting a job like mine. Some nights when he came home from work he closed and opened cupboards and doors with a resounding precision. We did a show together called *Cubist Cowboy Shootout*, based on a painting of Malcolm's, and took it back to

Auckland, and Brian danced in a concert of mine in New York. He nearly landed a great job but things just didn't work out. For a time there was a wall between us and I knew I was taking up too much space and casting a shadow.

Since Brian was five years old he knew he was going to die on 4 April 1984, at the age of twenty-seven. On the fateful day we made sure he was never alone to see if we could somehow prevent it. He worked until just before midnight and when the clock struck twelve he was still alive but he did return to New Zealand soon after that. Brian now lives in Sydney, Australia with his American/New Zealand/Australian accent as proof of his mangled lineage. There, he has come into his own as an actor and writer. I can sometimes see the top of his white head, now shaved, from the top of mine, and the occasional plumes of smoke as we exchange eruptions.

But that was later. At first all was exhilaration.

From our tiny balcony I could see the city spread out like an unwrapped gift. To the left, Lower Manhattan, the Statue of Liberty and the World Trade Center with its twin towers, and to the right, uptown, the Empire State Building and the intricately bevelled, silver-flashing minaret of the Chrysler Building. In between these peaks were thousands of smaller oblongs, all at different heights, carved and moulded out of red rock, brownstone, gleaming metals, black tar, all bristling with aerials, wires and flashing lights, with zig-zagging fire escapes and people hanging out of the windows. I felt like an eagle must feel, in its eyrie in the nook of a cranny in a city of mountains. In the deep canyons and ravines there were millions of people walking in never-ending streams: Native Americans, Puerto Ricans, African Americans, Italians, Slavs, Asians, Egyptians, Hasidic Jews, Anglo-Saxons, Polynesians, Caucasians; people ranging in colour from mayflower-white to ripe aubergine. And they were all moving so fast and talking so loud in a babel of languages, impelled by an energy that fizzed and popped in the air, that stepping onto the street was like jumping into a swift, powerful river. Except for the legless black man in a wheel-chair always on the corner of Broadway and Bleecker rattling a paper cup screaming, 'I need a million bucks,' and the Ginsbergian bums on the Bowery passed out in the gutters or huddled around fires in the urine-soaked snow, except for all the overgrown women pushing their lives in front of them in a shopping cart and the fiercely effeminate, swishy black teenager sitting in the middle of the road talking to himself on a toy pink telephone – except for them we were all going somewhere. Every few minutes the ground trembled and roared as silver-bellied, graffitied eels rushed even more people through a labyrinth of underground tunnels to their destinations. Human beings lived in the tunnels, with the rats and the thunder. In winter they lay over the gratings so the heated air could warm them, like giant abandoned babies, swaddled in newspapers.

To be a part of all this was made possible by my boss, Paul Taylor, the master-choreographer, on the day he hired me. I had only been in New York for a few weeks when I heard there was to be the first open audition for the Taylor Dance Company in four years. There were about 120 men vying for the one position and when I saw them all sleek and nervy, like thoroughbreds at the starting gate, I decided I didn't have a chance anyway so I might as well throw caution to the wind. My experience with Limbs performing in all kinds of situations gave me an adaptability the other dancers didn't have, and it became apparent right from the outset that Paul was drawn to me. As more and more of the thoroughbreds were cut I began to realise I had a chance. At the beginning it was specified that Paul was looking for a male 5 feet 8 inches or taller and at one point he walked around the room with one of the women from the Company, measuring us against her. When he got to all 5 feet $7\frac{1}{2}$ inches of me he said, 'You're not 5 foot 8 are you?' and I eyeballed him and replied, 'I dance 5 foot 8.' Paul raised his eyebrows at that and looked a little more closely at how I made up the missing half inch. On the last day of the three-day audition there were only two of us left, and when I was finally chosen it was as if I had been given the keys to the City. I was speechless with joy as the dancers in the Company welcomed me into their ranks.

In the words of the tribe of struggling dancers who I got to know in dance class, I 'lucked out'. Some of them had been working as wait-people for years, living on tips, waiting not only on tables but for the rare opportunity to audition for a place in one of the few full-time, well-paid, world-touring dance companies. They were like tireless mountain-climbers with the summit inside their heads, clawing for

73

a toe-hold on almost sheer cliffs. The inevitable knock-backs did not deplete their numbers; for every dancer who gave up, another two appeared. Most of them were relentlessly cheerful, certain that one day they would succeed. And I had walked in and somehow been given everything. Though many of my new dancer friends must have been envious, they cheered me on with an optimism and generosity distinctly American, as if they saw my triumph as tangible evidence that it could be done. I was one of them who had made it and, if me, why not them?

Paul was a shambling, hulking man of over six feet, in his fifties, wrapped in an air of overpowering wistfulness. He spoke in a tiny voice just above a whisper and the angrier he was the softer he spoke, so we had to lean closer and closer to hear. He cultivated an aw-shucks, Johnny Appleseed down-homeness and was always accompanied by Dee Dee, his decrepit dog, and a bottle of Mylanta for his gnawing ulcer. Though he was famous and successful in a city that worshipped fame and success he seemed bereft, as if he'd lost something crucial and knew he could never find it again. The day I got into the Company he took me to lunch and propositioned me, asking if he could be 'Diaghilev to [my] Nijinsky'. When I turned him down, pointing out that Nijinsky had gone mad, he smiled his aw-shucks smile and said, 'Oh well, that's okay.' Then I quoted to him, from memory, for reasons I have forgotten, the first lines of a favourite poem:

> I am not Scalene, old warrior with the shortened foot
> > hobbling by,
> nor isosceles prayer-pointing the sky,
> but part of the whole only, hypotenuse,
> my life stared at, paid away
> by the rightness of an angle's right eye.

This seemed to shut him up completely. He gave me a strange look and asked the waiter for the check.

When he was making a new work and things weren't going according to plan, Paul often needed a scapegoat; one dancer to carry all the blame, someone he could insult and ridicule. At the beginning of rehearsals there was always a frenzy of helpfulness, with everyone rushing to interpret and even to anticipate his wishes, anxious to avoid being singled out. All these conflicting suggestions and frantic efforts irritated him so much he became enraged and lashed out. I remember one day, after five hours of this, looking around the room and noticing we had all turned into a pack of nodding, cringing dogs, searching desperately for something to agree with, for a way to ingratiate ourselves with our wrathful master. The only time he tried it on me I gave him a look of such venom that he backed down and chose somebody else. After that we got on well. He contented himself with putting me on the rack and slowly teaching me how to dance as he once did. I think it was Paul's old boss Martha Graham who said that like a mystic a dancer dies twice; once when he or she stops dancing and the second, often less painful, death.

Paul made joyful dances, funny dances and dark dances. These categories sometimes overlapped slightly, but by an inner compulsion, he always, like Blake's *The Ancient of Days*, separated the dark from the light. The wracked, doomed relationships he was adept at creating could never be found in his joyful dances. In these works, gravity was dispensed with; only in the adagio section a note of aching loss was allowed to seep in. But never the anger and despair that his dark works released. I gave my all in his dances. To be one scintillating particle in the dazzling structures Paul built was a gift. I leapt in his sun, grovelled in his muck, and made my body shake so violently I think it satisfied even him.

There was an old tramp who used to wander around the East Village with a pack of docile-looking labradors, at least ten of them. The dogs were all brown and old, the same colour and vintage as him, and they seemed to take care of this man, who wore an arrangement of plastic bags tied together with string. Just down the street from my building there was a funeral parlour with an awning that led from its front door to the edge of the sidewalk. One day as I was walking past I saw the tramp and his dogs coming down the street and at the same time the funeral parlour's door opened and four sombrely dressed men emerged carrying a coffin. As they proceeded to the waiting hearse, in a straight line, it was as if the old man walked right through them and the dogs slowly followed in his wake under and around the coffin and the pallbearers. There was no collision or change in pace or even acknowledgement from either party, just this enormous feeling of ceremony as their paths crossed.

Next door to the funeral parlour was another door that led up one flight to the Club Baths. Often in the weekends, after dark, there was a line of men snaking down the stairs waiting to get in. Once you paid the man behind the grille you entered a world that has since disappeared. There were two or three floors of dimly lit amusements; a pool watched over by the obligatory replica of Michelangelo's *David*, a bar, a steam room and sauna, showers, a video room, an orgy room and cosy crawlspaces where men went to crawl. There were also long murky corridors, with doors at regular intervals. Behind these doors were tiny rooms, just enough space for a platform with a plastic-covered slab of foam to lie on. Sometimes these doors were closed, sometimes they were ajar (the differing amounts of openness signalling the differing degrees of availability), and sometimes wide open and half-naked men were lying, like tentacles, trying to attract someone better-looking than themselves. If you got there early enough you could hire one of these rooms; if not you made do with a locker and hoped to meet someone who had a room to go to. Once inside you could have been in any of the gay baths in New York. The unbridled testosterone, the eternal thumping music, the grunts and moans and sounds of flesh slapping and ramming together acted like a drug that changed my metabolism. Some nights I went to several baths and it was as if I entered the Club Baths on 1st Avenue and came out hours later from the exit of the Broadway Baths on 49th Street with no memory of the journeys in between.

In crowded cities, in public, there is an unspoken etiquette. The empty space between 6 inches and a foot around each person is sacrosanct. If the person is considered mad or dangerous, the space is greatly increased. For varying sums of money, extra distance can be rented, purchased or sold. If people are in a crowded place, like the subway, they allow the 'don't fuck with me' zone to shrink. In rush hour when people are crammed together, the rules change. It is then permissible to have clothed bodies pressed against each other as long as the palm or pads of the fingers of the hand of any person does not touch any part of another. Of course there are cases where people grope and allow themselves to be groped. This is like stealing, or allowing your pocket to be picked. In a crowded subway car all the neutral space is occupied by glazed, vacant looks. Some people whip out their books and read. In the baths all these rules change. Men walk past each other and stare, they let their hands lightly graze the torso or towel-swathed crotch of anyone they desire. There were men and youths in the baths I would never usually meet. Puerto Rican thugs, black husbands from Harlem, men it would be dangerous to even look at in the street. They were the ones I wanted, above all, to be underneath. Here they prowled the corridors, within reach. To touch them and be touched by them was, for me, a transgression of inhibitions so powerful I had to be drunk, but not too drunk, to let myself do it. One night at the Club Baths a 23-year-old Puerto Rican called Eric came up behind me as I was standing in the doorway of the video room and as we both watched the gods on the screen ravishing each other he gently reached out with his foot and put it right next to mine, just touching. Eric had a mouth that needed kissing in the same way a naughty child needs disciplining. When we tried to transplant our relationship from the hothouse atmosphere of the baths to the outside world, at first it wilted. Eric lived in Queens and his friends and family thought he was straight. Even in my neighbourhood where he was a stranger, if we were on the street and there were any Latinos about and I touched him at all he became sullen, then distant. But he called me *papito lindo* which I found out means 'pretty little father' and he loved to tease me by pointing out beautiful blond boys on bicycles that he thought were gorgeous. He stood me up many times but even if I got angry and called it off, a few weeks later I'd run into him at the baths and his mouth would pout and sulk and curl up at the edges, giving a potted history of my paddy, and we'd start all over again.

I first met Tobias Schneebaum at a dinner party in the Chelsea Hotel in the apartment of a composer who had written the music for *Runes*, one of Paul's works. Initially I wasn't keen to go but over the phone the red-headed Gerald enticed me with stories of Tobias's strange and exotic life. He told me Tobias had written a famous book about his experiences living with a primitive tribe of cannibals in Peru and that Tobias had himself eaten human flesh. Since that first trip, Gerald went on, Tobias lived with several different Stone Age tribes, mainly in New Guinea, and had slept in the men's-house, having ritualised sex with the headhunters.

At dinner I discovered Tobias was a mild-mannered, slightly stooped, Jewish man in his mid-sixties with an aura of extreme gentleness. I was in no way physically attracted to him but was fascinated by the discrepancy between his exploits and his appearance. He seemed almost frail but there was something monumentally patient about him, and with his protuberant hooded eyes, hovering smile and slow way of turning his head he reminded me of a giant and friendly lizard who had swallowed something immense and was basking in the sun, letting it go down. When he discovered I was from New Zealand, Tobias asked me if I knew of a New Zealand writer called Janet Frame. Janet has been my icon ever since I got my first library card. When I discovered her books, as a boy growing up in rural New Zealand, I knew nothing of her life. I couldn't understand all that I read but the words flashed and sparkled in my mind like clusters of jewels set against a crushing darkness, with the word Death as the central diamond. The rumours regarding her years spent in mental hospitals under 'forced custodial capture', her reputation as a complete recluse, the disagreements about the meaning and even the quality of her books and her famous, adamant refusal to discuss them, all these facts and half-facts I slowly gathered over the years, added to my obsession with all things 'Janet'. I wrote to her to thank her for her books and, unbelievably, she wrote back. I even spoke to her on the telephone but had yet to meet her in the flesh. In another, later letter I told her I was leaving to study in New York and said that perhaps I'd meet Turnlung, a character from *Daughter Buffalo*, one of her novels. In the book, Turnlung is an elderly, male writer from New Zealand who travels to New York and meets a young American man, a medical graduate studying death. They make love and adopt a newborn buffalo in the Central Park zoo as the child of their union. I got Janet's reply just before I left. On the last tattered sheet of her 'daffodil paper' she wished me 'all good fortune' and said that I might indeed meet Turnlung, or one of his kind.

So when it turned out that Tobias had spent one summer with Janet at Yaddo, a writers' colony in upstate New York, and that they had eaten breakfast together every morning, becoming firm friends, I felt at once that I had found Turnlung. As I remember it, at that moment the other guests at the dinner party vanished completely, as in one of those endlessly rehearsed quick scene changes in dance or theatre when a vibrant group covering the entire stage is within the space of a heartbeat seamlessly dissolved into a spotlit intimate duet, leaving Tobias and me wrapped up in the beginning of a conversation that has lasted for twenty years.

Tobias's studio apartment was in Westbeth, on West Street in the farthest western reaches of Greenwich Village. The monolithic brick building was specifically for artists, with art-controlled rents, and the apartments were eagerly sought after. Inside there were seemingly miles of white-painted hallways that all looked exactly the same, with door after identical door, each with a number. Many times I got lost, or ended up on the wrong floor looking for Tobias. The hallways were like tunnels inside one of those fake icebergs you see at the zoo, the ones with nicotine-stained, psychotic polar bears pacing back and forth. But I always found Tobias at the end of the maze.

The wall of windows at the end of his one big room overlooked the Hudson River and the piers, one of Manhattan's most notorious outside cruising areas. The light from the windows was filtered through a thicket of plants growing in pots that was as impenetrable and densely woven as the canopy in the jungles Tobias had found himself in. The walls and shelves were crowded with books, carved shields, spirit-poles, totems, magic fetish objects made from human bone, the feathers of rare birds and beads, and a dozen or more decorated human skulls. These were ancestor skulls given to Tobias by their descendants, the Asmat, a tribe of head-hunters in Irian Jaya that had adopted him. We drank white wine that Tobias decanted into carafes, ate the dinners he cooked, and to save him from coughing I gave him 'shotguns'; blowing marijuana smoke that had already been in my lungs through his greedily sucking mouth into his.

Tobias never tired of describing the elaborate penis sheaths, gourds, and piercings worn by the Asmat. And he explained to me their conviction that by eating the bodies of conquered enemies they also gained their strength. But his favourite subject was the Asmats' belief that the more sperm a man ingested through ass-fucking and cock-sucking the more powerful he became. As part of their initiation every adolescent male was assigned a kind of uncle, chosen by his parents to ritually fuck and be sucked by him. Most adult men, Tobias explained, even after they married had a lifelong male sexual partner called an *mbai*, and he himself had been given such a friend. All the men slept together in a men's-house, completely separate from the women. He said the words *ass* and *cock*, *fuck* and *suck* in a tone of such evangelical fervour and vehemence I felt the words were weapons being ritually blessed. He projected slides of his adventures onto the wall. One of them showed a sea of black faces with Tobias at the exact centre, not drowning in the black waves but by virtue of being taller, rising up out of them like a lighthouse. We drank and smoked so much that night that when I arrived the next time and Tobias opened the door stark naked, I was surprised to learn it had been my idea. And once I had given in to his desire for sex with me it was difficult to renege. I felt he was trying to swallow me and his mouth made me think of the fact it had eaten human meat. Besides, I wanted lovers my own age. So I gradually weaned him off me by allowing him slowly diminishing access to what he thought was now his. Even the carnivorous goodnight kiss became a bitter contest. We finally reached an uneasy truce but after that Tobias always considered me his lover and was scornful of all my other boyfriends.

I thought he was the bravest person I had ever met. He could never quite explain what made him walk into the jungle in Peru in 1955 in search of a tribe no white person had ever seen. The only direction he had was to 'keep the river on your right', later the title of his book. Equally astonishing to me was how, after several days' walking, when he felt himself surrounded by immobile, watching presences that he at first mistook for strange red blossoms, he walked up to one of the men and put his hand on his shoulder. I wanted to know how he felt as the cannibals tore his clothes off, as they caressed him, as they laughed and played together in a kind of frenzied reunion. But from the way Tobias looked at me it was clear that though it was beyond words, he knew I already knew the answer.

We were both delighted that the exact time in 1956 when he finally emerged from the jungle to tell his story to a world that considered him dead, I was being born.

– 7 –

The road to nowhere

The Company was a family, with Paul as the father and Bettie de Jong as Paul's right-hand mother. Bettie was Dutch, though she had grown up in Indonesia. She had been with Paul for over thirty years, firstly as a dancer, then, for a millisecond, as a spurned lover and now, apart from a cameo appearance in *Esplanade*, she was the rehearsal director. Paul rarely came on tour with us so it was left to Bettie to watch each performance and give us our notes. I can still see her with her glasses pushed back on the top of her blonde head, cigarette in one hand, yellow pad in the other, reading in her guttural hybrid accent the list of our faults, crossing them off as she went. Bettie punctuated her litany with jokes, encouragement and cackling laughter, negotiating the minefield of egos as best she could. She was

85

in her fifties, tall and thin, with long, fine hair tied back in a ponytail and there was an unbending quality about her, as if her insides had been scooped out and something foreign put back in. She was like a ventriloquist's doll that very occasionally strayed from the script. It was Paul's wishes she represented, Paul's dances she weeded, and if things didn't look how he wanted it was Paul who was offended. She was married but her life was devoted to the Company. Her husband Victor, with his courtly manner and even thicker accent, was like the ambassador of an unknown country that existed only on paper to appease some obscure uprising. I always had the strange idea that like a costume or a piece of stage scenery, Bettie was stored in a cupboard when she wasn't needed.

I was the baby of the Company and with my 'great accent' I was a novelty at first. Like all families there were rivalries and cliques. Jim was the baby before me. He was Fred Flintstone to my Barney Rubble. With black hair, twinkling eyes, a loud jokey voice and a face-splitting grin, Jim was the epitome, to me, of all things American. Although Paul favoured me over Jim he never complained and when

I rejected him in bed he just kept on trying and, when he got the chance, tried to steal any of my boyfriends that got within stealing

distance. Jim was a 'trouper'. He had a lover called Bill, but being on tour was a different world. Almost all the gay men in the group, including myself, at one time or another slept with each other.

When I was a child I wanted to run away and join the circus. Travelling around the world with the Company was, at first, like living in a fairytale. We moved from city to city, country to country, theatre to theatre. Each night the curtains opened or went up and we performed our rituals to a dark, glittering abyss. Under the lights it was impossible to see any individual audience member, even if we had time to look, which we didn't. But I could hear them clearing their throats, coughing, laughing, whispering and in some places even yelling things at us. At the end of each dance there would be a brief moment of complete silence before the applause came crashing over us in waves as we bowed, often with cheering and whistling, then subsiding to a trickle before rising up again as we milked them. In Germany the audience clapped in time like a stomping advancing army and in Paris once they booed us. As soon as a performance began it was possible to feel how the crowd was responding, as if it was a single unified sea monster, with each of its fronds waving and signalling back as our movements reached it. When it was transfixed, there was a sucking sound, like the sound a seashell makes when you listen to it. In some theatres there was limited space in the wings, so spare dancers stood out of sight to catch us as we hurtled off, as if the stage was spinning and the further we got from the centre in our complicated, criss-crossing patterns, the faster we went. Sometimes Bettie didn't go 'out front' but sat in the wings instead, and although I'm sure she was taking notes I always remember her sitting calmly on a wooden chair doing her embroidery or crochet-work as bodies hurtled past. When I think of the other dancers the first thing that comes to mind is the way each person moved. Like a fingerprint or the sound of a voice, each dancer was completely different. You could tell someone's life story from the way they interpreted the music. Whereas Kate pounced on the note and Chris ever so slightly preceded it, I tended to tease the beat as if I might be late but then at the last moment wouldn't. Linda bounced lightly on top of the music like a dragonfly skimming a pond, Eli flattened the note and Sandy sort of kicked it. There were as many ways of being on the beat as there were dancers. There is always an element of danger in a live performance and when the unforeseen occurs, legends are some-times born. Like the time Eli had a terrible cold and his huge beak of a nose was leaking mucus. He was facing upstage, his back to the front, dancing slowly with Monica, who was facing the audience, when in a pause in the choreography he looked up at her and said in his Lebanese/New York accent, 'I'm sorry, Monica,' and then blew his nose thoroughly on the front of her skimpy, floaty costume. This happened before I joined the Company but I feel as if I saw it. The stories were handed down, filled out and added to by each generation of dancers. After the performance we went out drinking, eating, getting high and talking, always talking. In the evenings Bettie drank vodka and wine. When she was 'in her cups' her voice curdled and she told stories of a time before any of us, a time when Paul was dancing and they went on no matter what and if you mentioned the name of any dancer who wasn't present she would repeat the name in a commiserating groan, nodding her head and tapping the side of her nose. The last stage of her drunkenness was the snarl. One night in Barcelona, after a performance in which I accidentally hit a light as I exited, Bettie turned on me at the party afterwards and slurred in her accent, 'And you with your fancy accent, you think you're so great . . .' before Jim led me away. But mostly Bettie and I were pals. I think she must have recognised the Bettie in me.

Every spring we had a three- or four-week New York season at City Center Theatre on the Upper West Side, rotating up to five different programmes, performing Tuesday through Saturday night with a matinée on Sunday. We had live music for these seasons and the sound of the orchestra warming up combined with the rumble of the gathering audience filtered into our dressing-rooms like pure adrenalin. The dressing-rooms were stacked on top of each other on three floors, with the more junior members of the Company higher, in the ones furthest from the stage. There was an old-fashioned elevator with a sliding grille door, with a matching diminutive old man whose name I've forgotten ferrying us up and down. Each dance was like a blossom that attracted a swarm of human insects or birds of the same colour, plumage and style and we crowded buzzing into the elevator, eager to pollinate. It was like living in a tiered doll's house, or a hive, always entering from the backstage entrance. I had a rule for myself that even if I wasn't dancing in a certain work I'd never go out front and watch because if I did I would realise how terrifying it was to be 'up there'. So I lived in the doll's hive going down in the elevator in my costume, numb with fear, then after dancing in the dazzling void of the stage for the watching giants, went back up all sweaty and relieved, either kicking myself for any mistakes I'd made or quietly soaking in an indescribable exultation. Afterwards I'd go out and thoroughly unwind.

In Copenhagen, in a castle, I saw a painting that intrigued me. It was hundreds of years old and was painted on a surface that was pleated. If you looked at it from one side it was the portrait of a woman, some long-dead princess, but as you walked to the other side that image withdrew as if the princess was closing the vertical slats of a Venetian blind she was standing behind and another person, a man this time, was opening his. This second portrait was of the matching prince. I suppose they must have been married but unusually for me I didn't read the caption. I was so fascinated by the ingenious *trompe-l'oeil* I kept walking back and forward in front of it, marvelling at its trick.

When I had first been chosen by Paul after the intense audition the sense of triumph was so acute it overruled any misgivings. My mother wept when I called her with the marvellous news and the sound of her crying was so close we could have been in connecting rooms. Malcolm was all for my new career. He was the one who helped me escape from an underworld of drugs and petty crime when I met him at the age of twenty-one. Five years on we were still supposedly together but now thousands of miles had come between us. We planned for him to come and join me but underneath I think we both knew it was a pipe-dream. My first full year in Manhattan was 1984; George Orwell had put a hex on that date and I remember having a fit of superstition when I realised that because I was living on the corner of 1st Avenue and 3rd Street, on the 13th floor, my address in space was emphatically the number 13, and in time, 1984. But these twin bad omens and the distant rumblings of a mysterious gay illness were mere background noise easily drowned out by the thunder of acclamation.

In Rome at the Vatican I saw a row of confessional booths that each had a priest waiting hidden within with a sign outside telling which language you could confess your sins in. There was a pornographic video store in Times Square which had similar booths with bilingual hustlers lurking outside who I found much more inviting.

A contemptuous black man wandered up and down a narrow aisle giving change. Once inside a booth you had to feed quarters into the slot to keep the gay porn playing. A quarter lasted for only about a minute and if you stopped a red light came on outside and the man would rap on the door and yell. Only one person at a time was allowed in the booths but our belligerent guardian turned a blind eye when it suited him and if you paid $20 most of the swarthy priests would absolve any sin. The booths were tiny, like upended coffins, and sometimes it was as if the video that was playing was an avaricious mirror reflecting what we were doing.

One night as I left and found myself standing outside on the street for some reason I just leant against the wall as if I was soliciting. There were prostitutes of both sexes working the beat and I knew what I was doing was dangerous. I had no intention of selling my body to anyone and I can't explain why I was standing there. I had done this years before in Sydney but now that was all supposedly behind me. It was as if the me that was standing there was still cracking it in Sydney and needed to be picked up and paid for by the me that was now the purchaser. This *doppelgänger* waited there patiently, in harm's way, for a long time. It could hear the commotion as the denizens of this particular precinct began to notice someone was trespassing. Finally a light-skinned, freckled black man with ginger hair came up and dragged me out of the trance I was in by telling me I'd get hurt if I stayed there. He took me home. This incident was part of the dark side of my new life I tried to hide from myself in a mist of drunkenness. I thought it was just a question of which side of the picture I was most conscious in but I soon discovered my pathetic attempt at *trompe-l'oeil* had repercussions.

I started to be afraid, as if the plane was going to crash. As if there was going to be a fire in the subway. Once I had to get Jim just to lie on me, on the floor of our dressing-room, so I wouldn't fly away. Then anywhere at all, without warning or discernible reason, my palms would begin to sweat, my mouth would dry up and my heart would palpitate like an alarm clock ticking faster and faster. Noises far away came close and the person right in front of me seemed to be behind

a thick pane of glass, so distant I could never reach them. If I was out in public my main concern was to hide the panic and I tried with all my might to act normal. But, once started, nothing I did could slow down or stop the tsunami of fear. I remember being trapped in the subway, with the train stuck in a tunnel, and darting quickly from car to car, shaking my hands so I wouldn't explode. One night I had such a severe attack I kept blacking out and at one point my chest was contracting and releasing as if a giant robot with steel pincers was squeezing me, then letting me go and squeezing, then letting go but when I finally went to the Emergency Room, they couldn't find anything wrong with me.

At the baths, things became strange. Sometimes the doors to the cubicles were wide open and the utterly available, skeletal bodies laid out on the pallets made me wonder if I had inadvertently opened a secret connecting door and had wandered into the funeral parlour. I knew there was a 'gay cancer' out there, but I had pushed the thought so far to the back of my mind it had come full circle and was now right in front of me. One night I found myself watching a man's face while another man's penis pistoned in and out of his mouth. The room was full of men all reverently watching and it suddenly struck me as the most hilarious thing I'd ever seen and I began laughing and laughing until a beautiful black man called David took me out and up onto a swaying, tinkling roof-garden where, before that night, I had never been. On week nights I drank beer and smoked dope but on the weekend it was vodka, which seemed to make me invisible and impervious to danger, like a somnambulist. I entered a subterranean, tunnelling world where men enacted venom-milking rituals in rooms almost pitch black, somewhere deep in the bowels of the earth. Once my eyes adjusted I could see as well as feel, smell and hear the groping shadows. Then my body seemed to gradually dissolve until I was just one hovering eyeball drifting through veils of smoke. I watched as a great, pulsating monster of conjoined flesh somehow squeezed out of its orifice a single masturbating boy and held him aloft as it moaned its encouragement in a many-throated roar. And there was a man hanging in a sling with another man elbow-deep in his rectum, as if a vet was helping a distressed animal give birth. I saw someone bent over a chair with his pants around his ankles, his naked arse in the air. He was like a half-skinned rabbit, looking over his shoulder, a startling detail in a painting by Hieronymous Bosch, waiting for anyone to do anything. There were holes in the black walls and out of these holes severed, moving body parts floated disembodied in the air, like the dismembered fragments of one butchered body trying to find each other to reconnect. In another cave-like space a group was intent around something. There was a naked man lying on his back on a pool table. Another clothed man was bent over him, slowly and methodically pinching the naked man's skin between finger and thumb and then lifting it up and equally methodically piercing the flesh with a steel needle, then letting it go and moving along to the next piece of flesh. By the time I got there he had already pierced at intervals of about six inches all down one side of the man's body and was starting on the other side. The man lying there was bristling with steel. As each needle was pushed through, the white, chilly skin flinched and quivered and shivered as if his nervous system was short-circuiting and then he sighed. We all sighed. The whites of his eyes flickered like the upraised eyes of an ecstatic saint in a nest of fire. While I was watching, my body came back as if each needle that pierced the man was bringing the same part of me back into the room. I stood in the corner and began to dance to a music that was so low and sinister it was like the slowed down, played backward sound of Tibetan monks chanting from *The Book of the Dead*. But it turned out that dancing was the only thing banned here and the man behind the bar kept coming out and telling me to stop and I kept saying okay and then once he'd gone I started again until they threw me out.

Sometimes in the morning after a night right out I couldn't remember any of it; just brief but vivid vignettes as the fog lifted and a vague memory of stumbling home like an exhausted caveman; head down, the rhythm ten steps more this way and a fall to the left, a block of straight-ahead staggers, a fall to the right, then blocks more of staggers on and on into the dark till I fell on my bed. It was as if my body knew how to take me home and I simply had to let it. Every morning I woke up hung over and with a feeling of dread but after doing class the night's booze was sweated away and by the end of rehearsal I was ready for more.

As well as dancing full-time with Paul I was doing my own concerts. I roped in anyone I could. Debbie, an old friend from Limbs, came all the way from New Zealand; even Tobias danced in my work. In 1984 I made *Dog Dance*, a drama of dominance and subjugation in which I was the dog and Tobias was my master. I had been obsessed with dogs since my own childhood pet had been run over by a neighbour. It is odd that he was called Toby. In rehearsals, from all fours, I barked out commands to Tobias, my master, as he kept forgetting where to go next. But in performance he was riveting, and when at the end he had to eat pâté from a dogfood can, there was a sharp intake of breath from the audience. One review said, 'Samuel Beckett would have loved it.' Would he?

In fact my 'career' was flourishing. Paul was giving me bigger and

bigger parts and whispered to me that soon, soon, he was going to make something especially for me. I think he knew even before I did that I wanted to leave. In the process of becoming a Taylor dancer, my body was being trained out of its own way of moving; it was becoming Paul's instrument, a kind of glove-puppet, and I began to sense that if I wanted to make my own work, I had to get out. It irritated me that Paul made dances idealising heterosexual relationships and I longed to make something that would be a slap in the face. After seeing the work of Pina Bausch, Sankai Juku and others I knew dance could do anything, go anywhere, there were no rules.

Paul had been to my first concert and assured me I had no talent for choreography, but I knew I had to make things. It was halfway through an eight-week tour of Spain, in Figueras, after a visit to the fried-egg covered Dali Museum, that I finally posted him my letter of resignation, giving a year's notice.

Spain was a country I had never been drawn to, but on that tour I was seduced by its ravaged grandeur, by Goya, and by the smell of blood on the wind. We performed on stages built in the ruins of

Roman amphitheatres, with colossal marble statues of Demeter and Ceres blindly overseeing us. One amphitheatre had been used to stage mock battles and, we were told, was flooded with water at the climax of the entertainment, drowning the slave-actors for the audience's enjoyment. As we put on our make-up in the bowels of this stone enclosure we all felt our flesh creep. We travelled in a bus from Barcelona to Madrid, from Segovia to Vallidolid, past fields of burning sunflowers, staying in medieval towns where the sun hammered the silent streets while small, dark people slept behind locked doors. They came out at night, in their finery, and stalked up and down the cobblestones like cats on heat. Restaurants opened at 10 p.m. and we performed at midnight. In one town Jim and I found a nightclub and when after a few drinks I wanted to leave, Jim asked me to wait while he had one last dance. He was intoxicated with joy and I stood and watched while he danced in a kind of frenzy to a song that became our anthem, 'Road to Nowhere' by Talking Heads. After we left the nightclub we wandered up a steep street with a bottle of bull's-blood wine and ended up sitting in the gutter with a pack of mangy pariahs. When a police car pulled up I was lying like a dog, with the dogs, sucking on the bottle and Jim hastily explained to the startled police that we were *Americano*, *bailarin*; they nodded understandingly, stroking their chins, and left us to it.

In Madrid I spent hours in the Prado Museum, with Bosch, Velazquez and Goya. There was one painting by Goya the colour of sand that at first glance was totally bare, uninhabited, like a colour-field abstract, but when I looked closer there was the profile of the head of a dog emerging from a darker brown smudge at the bottom left corner. It was looking up in mute supplication, drowning in quicksand. The painting was unbearably poignant; I would walk away and then have to go back to check if the little dog was any nearer its extinction. But it was always just about to be smothered, just about to transform the 1621 canvas into a twentieth-century abstract. Spain was like that, a defiant, haunting celebration of woundedness. When I told Angeles, our Spanish interpreter, of my love for this painting she attached herself to me. Angeles was less than five feet tall, but fierce, and with her blue-black hair, her stilettos, and *ratatat* voice, she towered over me. She was stern and immaculate, a Fascist's daughter, and I disappointed her deeply, but not before we translated each other's sense of humour. In my hotel room one night I showed her the treasured stone I had taken from Emily Dickinson's garden in Amherst. Then, when Angeles said, 'You're s-o-o romantic,' I immediately threw the stone out of the fifth-floor window and we both listened for a scream that never came. She looked at me with her bullfighter look, nostrils dilating, and said, 'You're VERY romantic,' then rang the bells of laughter in her belfry. On the long bus-trips we sat next to each other and I listened as she explained, in her guttural English, the complexities of her love life.

The tour was so long the Company fused into a kind of peristaltic organism, secreting and excreting whatever was necessary for its survival. At one climactic party we had in Madrid, Bettie stood in the middle of the small hotel room and begged us to throw cushions and pillows at her, to punish her for all the corrections she had been forced to give. So we did. Then she made herself as stiff as an ironing-board and we passed her around overhead while we drank and smoked and talked and laughed our forgiveness, under the Bettie-tent.

I sometimes think of the stone from Emily Dickinson's garden lying incognito on a street in Madrid, and wonder if it's had any new adventures since my grand gesture. I like to think Emily herself was not displeased when she heard of its parabola.

– 8 –

A bouquet

Back in New York, Tobias and I continued our symbiotic rela-tionship. He was my haven, my 'no spring chicken' cheerleader. He seemed to intuit the depths of my self-doubt and to make up for it, as if I were a religion, Tobias believed in me. He was writing a new book, *Where the Spirits Dwell*, in which I appear in a dream. I met all his friends and often went to dinner parties where I was the only one there under sixty. On my birthday he and his other best friend, the white-haired and exquisite Floriano, came into the room carrying in tandem a sliced-open watermelon blazing with 29 candles, singing 'Happy Birthday'. The red flesh of the melon and the miniature bonfire glowed in their eyes and cheeks as they advanced slowly towards me, warbling off-key.

The only time Tobias ever met my Puerto Rican lover Eric was on Fire Island and Tobias was so jealous he couldn't take his eyes off us. He cooked us a meal with so much salt in it none of us could eat it and when we went walking on the beach that night I had to stop him from running into the sea. It was all my fault because in the throes of Ecstasy I had sworn undying love to Tobias and had slipped a ring on his finger – a key-ring. He now thought we were married and with his accusing, wounded looks started to act like the wife that I secretly beat. After a terrible scene in which I called him a cancer to me we made friends and never broke up again. Eric however went out of my life almost the same way he came in. He brought his unsuspecting new girlfriend to one of my concerts and afterwards at dinner he played footsie with me under the table as we talked.

When *Te Maori* opened at the Metropolitan Museum I went with Tobias to a small party in honour of the elders who had come to guard their treasures. It was odd, sitting in their midst, as if I was back in the small town where I grew up. When I was little I somehow got the impression Maori were supposed to be inferior. In the centre of Tuakau, just off the main street, there was a fenced-off area where only Maori people went. I was never told about this place, it was just there. I first realised its existence when I was in the main street with Mum one day and unearthly sounds started coming from nowhere – a wailing and keening and singing that sounded almost inhuman, supernatural, as if it was the Waikato River that was singing. Mum explained that the Maori were having a tangi, or funeral, on their marae, and afterwards I saw old Maori ladies all dressed in black with green inlaid webs of moko on their chins, sitting in the gutter like dusty blackbirds, waiting for the bus. I remember trying to stare into their faces but they seemed to slide their faces away from me so I couldn't look. Now in Manhattan I was sitting with them. I started talking to an old man next to me and when he discovered where I was from he asked about my family. It turned out he had walked to school every morning over 60 years ago with my grandfather, who was now dead. He was so pleased he made a speech to the whole room about coming all the way to New York to end up sitting next to what he called 'a Tuakau boy' and then we all joined hands and sang 'Po kare kare ana' together and I felt my cynicism dissolve as I was immersed in the singing river. They were all starry-eyed innocence and when I asked them if they had seen much of New York they giggled and said, 'Oh no, we wouldn't go outside the hotel, we might get lost.'

The exhibition itself was a revelation. Far from home I saw the Maori in a different light. The venerated objects pulsated. They stood as tall as the Egyptians; one carving could have given birth to all of

Brancusi. This wooden post was *Uenukutuwhatu*, the tribal and war god of the Waikato tribes, where I am from. It was simple; a severe denuded koru, bristling with malevolence, with four spikes like stylised tongues of flame coming from the nape. This was the root of the wailing I heard as a child coming from the pa in Tuakau. I had had no idea. Also, there were two wooden burial chests so forbidding it was a challenge to meet their gaze. I felt I should stand to one side, out of self-protection. The power radiating from these objects helped me understand why they are regarded as living beings.

Somewhere on tour in Middle America Chris got shingles and one of the women refused to dance with him. Then in Germany Jim got sick. We were rooming together the day he went to the doctor. I was out somewhere; he had called a cab and when it came he forgot he'd left one of those little portable elements that plug into the wall in a cup of water on the floor. While he was gone the water evaporated, the cup broke and the element burnt a big hole in the carpet. The proprietor was very angry and made Jim, who was getting sicker and sicker, pay for the whole room to be recarpeted. That night while we were sleeping the heraldic *faux* bedhead that was screwed to the wall somehow unscrewed itself and fell like a nightmare on our heads. I tried to argue with the proprietor that surely this potentially dangerous mishap should be somehow quantified and deducted from the price of the burnt carpet but he was implacable. Jim struggled on and it was from Denmark that he was finally sent home.

In those days the way one actually contracted Aids was unclear; it was thought you could catch it from breathing the same air, or drinking from the same cup, anybody ill was taboo. Underneath a blanket denial a kind of witch-hunt smouldered and rumours spread like wildfire; Aids was voodoo from Haiti, swine-fever from Africa, those infected were to be rounded up and quarantined on an island, it was God's punishment and Ronald Reagan, with his just-say-no-Nancy, presided like a malfunctioning cyborg. Though I despised him, I found in Reagan an unconscious ally; his prolonged refusal to utter the word 'Aids' perfectly chimed with my own denial and it wasn't until late one night, at the end of a tunnel of drunk, when I came to a massive iron door, the door of St Mark's Baths, extravagantly barred and padlocked with a sign slapped on it yelling, 'Closed by order of the New York City Department of Health', that I finally allowed a glimmer of fear into my heart.

At first I was too afraid to go into Jim's room in Aarhus, where some of the girls were looking after him, but eventually I overcame my fear and was able to be with him as he waned. In Jim's last season in New York, Paul gave him the solo he had always wanted and I watched from the wings as he valiantly danced to Bach's 'Musical Offering'.

One year later, in my own last City Center season, for the first time ever Paul invited four of us, all men, to choreograph our own short solos to be included in the rotating programmes. He even suggested the music for mine. To the minuet from Ravel's 'Le Tombeau de Couperin' I created a dance called *Faun variations*. This work was the consummation of my identification with the legendary Russian dancer, Vaslav Nijinsky, who, in 1912, created the role of the Faun. His ability to jump and hover in the air was a gift I shared. There are no films of his work, only photographs and eyewitness accounts. His *L'après-midi d'un faune*, was a group work; he danced the title role and the choreography was in two dimensions, in profile, like Egyptian painting. This was revolutionary in that it revealed the profound expressiveness of immobility and a limited, almost pedestrian, movement palate. Less was more, at last. Also, for the first time, the dancers occasionally stood still while Debussy's music flowed like a stream around them. My rather banal idea was to release the Faun into the third dimension, using three or four of Nijinsky's poses as touchstones. I worked on *Faun variations* all the previous year and even when I wasn't physically rehearsing it I would take out the movement doodles in my head and fiddle with them in a kind of daydream, sometimes even seeing what should happen next. After unkennelling the dog inside in *Dog Dance*, I unwittingly made room for the Faun and the dance was a success; even Paul liked it. As I performed the work to an audience which on one occasion included my first and most loyal fan, my mother, and on another Mick Jagger, a part of me believed that with the help of the spirit of Nijinsky, I wasn't pretending to be the Faun, I was becoming it.

My own last concert was at the 14th Street 'Y'. We premiered *Hey Paris* and *Quartet* and I danced *Faun variations* again. Tobias had a starring role and Debbie taught the dancers a work I'd made for Limbs called *Halcyon*. Jaime, my new and final New York boyfriend, nailed the tricky solo in *Quartet*. It was a massive team effort and we were fêted. Paul stayed away and told me later he'd heard we danced completely naked. I still have a grainy hand-held video of our last performance. At the end when all fourteen of us lined up for our curtain call, I was in the centre and someone handed me a large bunch of white flowers. I got flustered, trying to be humble, and passed the bouquet to the surprised person next to me, who passed it on again. To the sound of crashing applause, the unwanted bunch of flowers was handed along the line of bewildered, smiling dancers to the end of the row, and as the video cut to black, it had started coming back my way again.

DOUGLAS WRIGHT and DANCERS

at

THE EMANU-EL MIDTOWN Y

344 East 14th Street, near First Avenue

Sat. & Sun., 6 & 7 June, 8 p.m.

— guess you already got one of these

Tickets $7 or TDF $2

Phone 673-2207 for reservations

Dancers:

Homer Avila	Chryssa Parkinson
Lisa Dalton	Sarah Perron
Mark Dendy	Leanne Plunkett
Gail Gilbert	Denise Roberts
Jaime Martinez	Manuel Rodriguez
Debbie McCulloch	Dennis Udall
Shona McCullagh	Douglas Wright *me*

and guests— do you remember

Love

Douglas x

P.S. that's my ass.

Photo: Emilio Segares

Malcom Ross
26 King St
Arch Hill,
Auckland
New Zealand.

Our building never had a doorman or any security and the long-time residents had always had an unofficial busybody unwelcoming committee set up at the front door. At first they had been friendly but over the years what began as polite enquiries as to the exact nature of my relationship with Yvonne, the designated tenant who had illegally sublet to me, turned into knocks on the door at night when I was stoned out of my mind by prying, peering, rat-like members of a tenants' committee. Brian had already left when I was eventually chucked out. In my last few months in the city I moved from sublet to sublet, the rooms gradually shrinking until at the end I was living in a kind of hallway with a photographer who later went blind.

Limbs wanted me back to dance and make my own work. Paul

106

didn't want me to leave and we agreed I would take a year's break and then decide. One of Paul's ex-dancers tried to talk me out of it, telling me, 'You look like you're being born up there,' and she was right. Most of the dancers I knew thought I was mad. They said if I stayed Paul would make me a star. A star in New York! But everything had changed. One sunny day I was so hungry for green I went to Washington Square Park and found a narrow space, just my size, on the grass and in the throngs of people I lay down. A bird flew over me and as it flew, for just an instant, I felt it, as if it was an amputated part of me that had been magically re-attached and I knew I had to go home. Tobias gave me his blessing and one of the decorated human skulls given to him by the Asmat, because I was now part of the family, leaving.

New York covered in a deep carpet of snow. New York with the sun so hot you stick to the tar on the road.

A very thin Jim and I sat in a restaurant where he told me about the crystal healers, the macrobiotic diet, the positive thinking, the wonder-drugs, but we both knew. We watched through the window as a tramp, a young black man, held a one-dollar bill delicately between thumb and forefinger over the grating of a gutter and nearly let it go, then in an elaborate pantomime of agonised indecision, he changed his mind and took it back from the edge. Then something came over him and he kept teasing, reaching the money closer to the hole, nearly letting it fall but stopping himself just in time again. Jim and I fell silent as the tramp continued his taunting game, sure of his audience. After many attempts he finally brought himself to the point of no return and let the dollar bill fall into the grating. Down it fluttered, like a severed wing, down into the sewers with the rats and the thunder, and then the vagrant, impeccable mime just walked away abruptly as if nothing had happened.

On my last night in New York I was having dinner with Jaime at a restaurant in St Mark's Place when we had a violent argument. I don't remember now what we argued about but I stormed off into the night blind with anger. I went to a park in Alphabet City that I knew was haunted by drug-dealers and approached one of the black youths that was slinking around in the darkness. I bought some crack from him and smoked it in a glass pipe there and then. It tasted like the exhaust fumes of a car but then the darkness we were sitting in opened up and I was rushed to a place of utter gladness, with the black drug dealer as my heavenly benefactor. He listened to my confession and then, just when I felt we were about to understand everything, I was rudely dumped back on the dark bench and his eyes were totting me up. I kept wanting more and ran up a small debt which the dealer then came back with me to collect. I don't remember his face; he was a shadow, a negative, like a black cat at night which is visible only when it blinks. On that last night I was staying in Westbeth, Tobias's building, in the empty apartment of one of his friends. After we walked in the door I left the man for a moment as I went to the bathroom. When I came out he'd gone, taking with him my wallet containing not only a couple of hundred dollars but also my passport. I ran through the maze of iceberg hallways trying to catch up with him but he was nowhere to be found. It was already 4 a.m., a black-and-whitemare, and my plane was leaving that afternoon. I woke Tobias and in the hideous morning we traipsed uptown to the New Zealand Embassy where we met Witi Ihimaera, at that time the Consul. He was wreathed in diplomatic smiles and without fuss issued me a document to say that I was, temporarily, me, so I could go home.

– 9 –

Shorn

The move from New York to Auckland was such an upheaval I had to leave before I left and arrive before I got here; as if the New York me was slowly dismantled then sucked into a migrating steel bird and after being sprayed, searched, stamped and officially welcomed, was slowly reassembled into the New Zealand me. The flight itself was arduous and terminally boring. Passengers were larval, cosseted in blankets in reclining incubators, fed intravenously by smiling hand-people, hypnotised into submission by Muzak and mindless movies.

Even though I had been back at least once a year the first sight, from the air, of the green-furred hills was always a shock. Where were the people? Were those really houses? How did it get so green?

It was like floating in a white cloud above a giant billiard table, with the moss-green felt tumescent and rolling. The folds and crevices affected me with an almost erotic intensity and the shadow of our plane knew no obstacle. It raced across the paddocks and roads, over the toy-houses, through the fences of the hidden people, leaping the veins of the mirror-flashing creeks, like a shape-shifting black rabbit headed for its burrow.

Malcolm's mother had died of cancer and with some of his inheritance he had gained a mortgage from the bank and was living in and paying off an old wooden house in Arch Hill, an inner-city suburb of Auckland. After the well-insulated, centrally heated, air-conditioned buildings of New York the bungalows in rainy Auckland were leaking, rotting sheds. Of course I was lucky to have a roof over my head at all but the fragility of the shelter combined with my emotional predicament made that time reminiscent of a night I spent once in a pup-tent in a raging storm with Rick, an old school friend. We kept waking up to find our tent had been blown away and no sooner had we found it in the dark, re-pitched it, got back into our sleeping-bags and fallen asleep than it would be ripped away again and so on until we were doing it in our shared nightmare.

I came back covered in glory. The two seasons I did with Limbs in 1987 and 1988 were, so I've been told, triumphs. But I was caught in a downward spiral that, fuelled by alcohol, swirled me to the brink. The company had changed completely. Whereas, before Brian, I'd been the only gay person, now it was full of muscly mincing Marys in skin-tight hotpants, waggling their perfumed fannies and calling each other *gurlfrend*. Though they welcomed me and worked hard, dance seemed to be less important to them than their hairstyles and I sensed my own 'hairdo' was alien. The hatefulness of their attributes seemed a kind of diagnosis of my own condition. No doubt it was all in my mind, and no harm was meant, but I felt like an interloper.

In *Now is the Hour*, my first evening-length work, I had a sheep shorn live on stage each night by a professional shearer. At first we only had the one sheep, in its little pen, in the wings, waiting for its moment. But we discovered it got lonely and sometimes baaed during the quiet bits, distracting the audience, so the shearer started bringing two sheep, to keep each other company. And then, when the chosen one was taken on stage to be shorn, the other one could be heard from the wings, bleating its abandonment. It became quite complicated. I think at one point there were three sheep in the wings. The work contained nudity and in Tauranga we were picketed by outraged Christians with signs warning, 'You can't pull the wool over God's eyes,' and suchlike. They got their picture in the paper.

At that time the only place I felt safe was onstage. There, at least, I had the illusion of control. To me dance is sacred and even at my worst, I never touched alcohol before a performance. Afterwards, though, I drank oceans of it. At the end of the opening night in Auckland the audience howled like a banshee. I was still shimmering with the glitter of overseas and they wanted to swallow me whole, or so it seemed. Another bouquet was handed to me at the curtain call and, in another grand gesture, I stepped forward and placed it dead centre, right on the throat of the stage, as an offering to the force that had somehow been unleashed.

I shared my role in *Now is the Hour* with Tai, one of the other dancers, and we alternated nights. He brought a quiet elegance to the role that I danced as a kind of self-immolation. I have a dim memory of spending the day up a tree in Christchurch, drinking red wine, egged on by the infamous Barbara Franks, and then going that night to watch the performance with a flask of gin. As I sat with a packed audience I yelled out loud, derisive comments, wolf-whistling at the serious bits and clapping enthusiastically at the poignant moments. I sat in the back row next to Barbara and the people in front of us kept turning round and staring at me in wonder. No one told me to shut up, or at least not that I remember. The dancers were not impressed.

Waking up the next morning, hung over, the split second when it hit me what I had done and that I had to go and get in a mini-van with all the dancers to drive to Dunedin was, I think, just punishment.

After that I sank fast. Malcolm, Debbie and other friends tried to help me but I was beyond their reach. Actually, I thought Malcolm was trying to kill me. I had an attack of shingles so painful it felt as if thousands of tiny needles were tattooing a fiendishly inclusive list of my sins, from the inside, while red-hot barbed wire was slowly rotated under my skin, piercing and burning the confleshion. The next stage was the formation of large blisters that looked like plastic shopping bags filled with water hanging in bunches on the left side of my chest and back and under that arm. It reminds me of a poem I used to know with the memorable line 'his pustules visibly festered'. As I lay in bed in agony, Istina, our tortoiseshell cat, sometimes sat on my stomach staring at me while I patted her harder and harder, then as hard as I could, to give her a taste of what I was enduring.

That Christmas I remember staying in somebody's empty house while they were away and drinking continually, crawling on my hands and knees in sheer terror because I felt people could see me through the windows. Even after the shingles had gone the pain was physical, an abscess of guilt, fear and grief and there was no poultice, no friendship or family that could relieve it. I went to a psychic who barricaded herself behind a wall of crystals before she would talk to me. She gave me a prayer to pray and asked me please not ever to think of her, because I was so toxic even my thoughts were dangerous. So I begged the purple flame to cleanse me and tried to keep my thoughts to myself but nothing helped. All I could do as the abscess rotted and finally burst was drink, cry, and read aloud poems by Emily Dickinson. A counsellor called Liese found me and sat and listened. She quite liked Emily too. Liese's Dutch accent reminded me of Bettie and with her help, when I was ready, she took me to a detox-house in Federal Street where I met people who drank detergent, a Neanderthal boy who had been picked up after he shat in the holy water font of an inner-city church, and others who, like me, were drowning. We got sober together. Once I got out I realised I couldn't go back to New York; I had to make my own way. I decided to form a company in New Zealand and from here to take my work to the world.

> Crumbs fit such little mouths –
> Cherries suit robins –
> The eagle's golden breakfast strangles them.
> God keeps his oath to sparrows
> Who of little love know how to starve.

Part Two

– 10 –

Off the map

All this mental travelling is exhausting and in between journeys, back
at headquarters, I rest on the couch. At times, as I lie there, it is
difficult to tell whether I am awake or asleep and as I hover on this
elastic boundary my mind plays delicious tricks. My resting place is
in the back unit of the last driveway at the end of a dead-end street
and at the bottom of my garden a small stream and a grove of trees
separate me from a public golf course. This looming forest of willows,
broom and conifers is supposed to screen me and my neighbours
from errant flying golf balls and is a kind of no-man's-land where
people, usually male, are always searching for their lost missiles.
During my frequent rests I can hear them calling out to each other;
'A little to the left!' 'No, behind that tree just next to you!' 'Have you

got it yet?' 'Found it!' and so on.

One day as I drifted in and out of a waking sleep these random sentences started to connect with something entirely unconnected that had lodged in my head. I had noticed on television that people kept saying, 'This'll put New Zealand on the map,' and 'This'll *really* put New Zealand on the map,' and 'Now, this has definitely put us on the map,' and, by the amount of times these phrases were repeated and the vigorous way they were said I realised that no matter how many times we were put on the map we kept slipping off it again. Now, somehow, in my levitating mind it was the television presenters and their interviewees who were wandering in the no-man's-land calling out to each other, searching not for lost golf balls but for our lost country which had been driven off the green.

That night when the six o'clock news came on the mother-and-father announcers sat on either side of a map of the southern hemisphere showing a huge, outsize New Zealand; and taking turns, smiling grimly, in cold blood they recited a litany of disasters at me. The international incidents were accompanied by extensive details regarding the New Zealanders who died in them, or were injured, or miraculously escaped, or were nearly there, or in some desperate cases even happened to be in the same country. It seemed to me in my morbid state that to die in a disaster overseas was a new and instantaneous way of giving New Zealand some much-needed visibility. These disaster-celebrities, if they survived, or their families, if not, were later produced on-screen and milked, live, of their tears by television personalities who were famous for something called human interest. The local victims of international disasters often turned out to have been very good at sport and to have loved life. And then I was reminded by the weather-lady what a great little country

120

we lived in, so safe, beautiful, clean and green; a land of the highest lows and the lowest highs and to get my woollies or sunhat out and then one of the flying golf balls hit the roof of my house with a loud thump which startled me out of the odd dream I was having to the sound of the wind in the trees.

– 11 –

Sky burial

A few weeks after telling me the first part of his bird-watching history Malcolm came back to visit and to continue our talk. The first instalment had unlocked vistas but to penetrate even deeper I needed to hear more. I felt like one of a set of twins separated at birth, who, when they finally meet, discover startling familiarities in their different stories, as if they had each been dreaming the other's life, and needed only to be prompted to remember.

Malcolm is the tensest person I've ever met. If I come upon him unawares I'm always careful to clear my throat, or softly whistle to avoid startling him. When surprised he makes a movement best described as a convulsion which then bounces off his body into mine like an electric shock. He calls it being 'twitched'. Malcolm is also a great yawner. When he stays he often yawns for hours on end, opening his mouth so wide he almost dislocates his jaw, making that yawning sound which when repeated sounds like a stag mooing. It's quite difficult not to moo in reply. That day he seemed even more nervous than usual. When he arrived, after one of his bone-crushing hugs he flitted about the room whistling under his breath. When I pointed it out he said he was unaware of it; it was subliminal, low and tuneless, as if the wind had unearthed a bone and was haunting it.

We took up our usual positions on the balcony on a spring day of such changeable temperature that during the two hours we sat there we both kept taking off layers of clothes then putting them back on again. Each change of clothing seemed to coincide with a twist in the story and I felt the weather was listening and adding its comments.

The school roll at Motukiore fell from 30 to 13 as Maori moved to the city and when Malcolm was 11 the family pulled up anchor and sailed to Poutu Peninsula. Poutu means cut off and at first sight Malcolm was so appalled by the barrenness of the place he burst into tears. It was flat and treeless, unfriendly, even threatening. In Motukiore the sky was kept apart by trees and pushed around by hills but now his cover was gone and the sky rushed in. He tried to transfer his physiognomy of hills onto the clouds but clouds haven't got time to sit for their portraits. The sky at Poutu was all-important, too big, and there was more sun, more rain, more wind; it was like standing on a line drawn by a ruler completely exposed to the previously unsuspected elements of erosion.

In the same way as autistic people study facial expressions so they can mimic the appropriate emotions, Malcolm has convoluted theories to explain the motives behind other people's unfathomable

From a sketch by Major-General G. Robley, after
the portrait painted in England in 1820.

Hongi Hika.

actions. In one of his more persuasive conclusions he believes his
mother became a church-historian because in 1931 when she was 11
and on a trip 'Home', she was sitting in a car with her brother outside
Belfast Cathedral when she noticed that every man who walked past
either lifted his hat at the church, or spat on the pavement. Malcolm
couldn't explain why but like his mother at the same age, in a
different place he felt compelled to find out why Poutu was so naked.
His mother had a library on New Zealand history and in one of the
books, *Maori Wars of the Nineteenth Century* by S. Percy Smith, he
discovered one horrifying reason.

MAORI WARS

OF THE

NINETEENTH CENTURY:

The Struggle of the Northern against the Southern
Maori Tribes prior to the Colonisation of
New Zealand in 1840.

BY

S. PERCY SMITH, F.R.G.S.,

President of the Polynesian Society, &c., &c.

SECOND AND ENLARGED EDITION.

CHRISTCHURCH, WELLINGTON AND DUNEDIN, N.Z.;
MELBOURNE AND LONDON:

WHITCOMBE & TOMBS LIMITED.
1910.

At the time when Malcolm's family moved to Poutu the Maori
Affairs Land Development Scheme was breaking in the land to re-
settle the absentee owners. Malcolm read that this tribe, the Ngati
Whatua, had fled after a bloody massacre in 1825 when the famous
chief Hongi Hika all but annihilated them in utu or payback for an
earlier battle where two of his brothers were slain. During the
massacre, named Te Ika-a-ranganui, in which nearly a thousand
Ngati Whatua were killed, Hongi wore the chain-mail coat of armour
and helmet given to him by King George IV on his visit to England
in 1820. His blind wife Turu-ka-tuku who 'always accompanied him

in his expeditions and whose advice he was said to constantly follow' stood on a ridge nearby with her attendants and watched the battle with her inner eye. At a decisive point, when the enemy was gaining, she called out a warning to her husband, urging him on, and in response Hongi struck hard, the tide turned and the battle was eventually won. Fleeing warriors were chased and killed in a rout and most of the survivors ended up in the Waikato where I come from. Many of the dead were eaten there and then, before they rotted, and those captured were enslaved. Apparently the victors travelled with these slaves as a kind of walking pantry, killing and eating one of them whenever they were peckish. The image of the blind seer with her long black hair levitating in the wind, calling out instructions to the chief-in-shining-armour, stuck in Malcolm's mind as the central riddle in a grisly fairytale. The book called it 'one of the most sanguinary battles ever fought in this country'. The mass slaughter was possible only because of the muskets made available by contact with Europeans. According to S. Percy Smith, Hongi had up to five hundred muskets while the Ngati Whatua had only two.

And there was a further level of absence. A primeval forest of giant trees had once stood here. Kauri live for thousands of years and as they extract the goodness from the soil they develop something called a podzole, a hard layer that looks like ironstone which as it spreads puts the nutrients beneath out of reach. In this way kauri are suicidal trees; once they have depleted the soil they die and it takes centuries before anything can grow where they've been. From the 1880s into the first part of the twentieth century the land was leased to Dalmatian immigrants who extracted the valuable fossilised kauri gum that lay scattered and buried in the scrubland like the frozen arteries of the massive forest that had disappeared. They worked communally, in groups of up to thirty, pecking and hacking at the earth with shovels and spears, and the amber-coloured gum was then sold to be used in making varnish and linoleum. These gumdiggers were famous for their ability to dig, their lives were harsh and they were hard men. I heard an old man on the radio who was a boy living near the gumfields in the early 1930s. His father was the local butcher and he described with relish how he delivered fly-blown haunches to the 'dallies'. According to him, they sometimes paid their bills in gum or curios. He said they heated the gum over a candle-flame and when it was malleable, inserted insects, even butterflies into the resin, mimicking the natural creation of prehistoric fossils. How they managed not to break the fragile butterfly wings was a mystery to him. It was dainty work for such burly men, but they were cunning, or so he said. I have found some such reminiscences iffy. Memory can sometimes be a sieve for atavistic prejudice; the creation of forged curios for the cabinet of history.

The Dalmatian gumdiggers were refugees from the Austro-Hungarian Empire and many were fleeing to avoid conscription in the occupying army. Viewed with suspicion as alien 'Austrians', they were largely ostracised by white New Zealanders, but found an unexpected welcome from another dispossessed people, the local Maori, who began to trickle back.

So the area was blood-soaked, ransacked and abandoned at least three times in living memory. Now herds of big machines were brought in to break up the podzole and fertilise the earth so it could become pasture for dairy farms. Poutu was made up of a plateau riddled with deep, swamp-filled gullies. The swamps were being drained and fences put up, the reclaimed land divided into economic units and most of the Maori lured back were saddled with huge mortgages they could never repay. They were slaves on their own land. The Maori kids Malcolm went to school with were descendants of the survivors of the massacre, and the Banecovich, the Jarecivich and the Mattich families were the great-great-grandchildren of the union between the gumdiggers and their Maori women. Malcolm knew more about why they were here than they did, but describes it as a forced discovery, as if these vanished events were being transmitted through the ether of the years and he was involuntarily tuned to their frequency. But with this knowledge the sky did become more manageable. It didn't shrink; he just found a way to relate to it, to see its possibilities. Poutu was flat but the flatness was deceptive; the gullies were plunges into depths. In the upper reaches of the Okaru Gully there was a single giant kauri which Malcolm thought of as a lone remnant of pre-history. He sort of prayed to it, though he would never have used that word. His parents believed in a divine rationalism that had disproved the invisible.

They lived right on the rim of Okaru Gully, a deserted canyon. One morning he remembers lying in bed looking out his bedroom window and watching a wind-blown sandhill slowly spilling into the gully and it struck him as such a strange, exciting phenomenon that he ceased to feel banished from the old landscape.

Poutu was hawk country. He used to go down to the bottom of the gully and lie on his back and watch them come in and out of the sky. When hawks are courting they perform a mesmerising double-spiral flight, ascending as they go. What entranced Malcolm was the rhythm; as they come towards each other they seem to speed up then continue languidly to the outer reaches of their individual loop before curving and swooping in faster again. As they were enacting this aerial mating dance they went higher and higher until they were mere specks on his retina, a disappearing double helix, and if he hadn't watched them from the beginning he wouldn't have been able to see them at all. All the time they made a piercing scream which Malcolm wrote as 'ker'. Somehow he found that Okaru Gully had wonderful acoustics and if you lay at the base of one of the cliffs your voice projected upwards better. He began to imitate their scream, with no other motive than mimicry at first, but gradually found he could draw a hawk out of the sky, even from the tiniest speck. Hawks have superb vision and they usually glide at about 60 metres for small prey but they are better equipped to detect movement than pick out a stationary body. Anything still is a potential meal and they probably wouldn't have any scruples about scavenging on a dead human as opposed to a sheep. Lying completely still and calling out to them in their own language Malcolm could get them to come within about 15 metres of him but then they saw his mouth moving and would swing away on a heavy clambering of wings. Hawks are clumsy on the updraft. If he could have called them without moving his lips they might have come right down and made a meal of him. Anyway he could never repeat the scream after his voice broke.

Every morning before school Malcolm collected the milk from an old Maori; Uncle Andrew was an honorary uncle. He was a master of silence and always looked over Malcolm's head with his clouded eyes as if seeing distant phenomena. The proper ceremony lasted two minutes before he handed back the billy. He knew Malcolm scampered all over the countryside but didn't object. From Muarangi, Malcolm could see enormous tracts of country, a hundred miles in either direction, with the relentless Tasman at his back, and there would often be up to six scrub fires burning in the distance. These were deliberate burn-offs. As he lay there watching the fires burning, under his elbow were fragments of charred human bone he'd even then learnt to identify as not cow or sheep. Great plumes of smoke swelling into the sky from a long way away were to him as pungent as sexual fantasy.

At 12 Malcolm left home and went to board at Northland College in Kaikohe for the next five years. He was then out of his father's reach, except for holidays when the violent tutorials continued. One evening, just before he left, his mother inadvertently cured him of his incontinence by saying across a roomful of people, after Malcolm had refused a cup of tea, 'Don't worry, you won't wet your bed.' He was humiliated but she was right and he never wet his bed again. It was the only time she ever referred to it in his entire childhood. That was one major worry crossed off the list, but by this point fear was, for him, as natural as holding his breath. His brother had already been at Northland College for two years. When Malcolm first got there he was so frightened he didn't shit for a week. The chief focus of his terror was the sliding door between the dining-room and the kitchen which had to be closed at the end of each meal. This door was extremely heavy and some of the third-formers were too small to move it without help. The boy chosen by roster to close it was watched by 130 other boys and the combined weight of all those looks added to the door's gravity. Malcolm had no real reason to fear the task because he was big enough to do it but for him the door was inherently evil. They slept in dormitories of eight or twelve with each bed containing a boy from each year, in regimental order, from the dormitory's head down to the lowest rank, like knives, forks and spoons set out for the formal meal of sleep. It was like being in the army and all his waking life was measured to the minute. Malcolm thinks he went mad in the last two years of school. He remembers getting regular letters from his mother that were like echoes of his own nagging worries, long lists of questions and remote-control commands. 'Have you seen the dentist?' 'Don't forget your shoes.' He imagined her sitting at her typewriter in the empty house in the middle of a paddock tapping out these messages that seemed a shorthand or code for something she couldn't bring herself to say. A particularly urgent misdemeanour occasioned a telegram which read, 'Wash spelling.' It was odd that when he became a senior and no longer had to close the door in the dining-room it was as if he had lost the one thing that anchored him and he became untethered, filled with a sense of loss, and would take off at night, crying and wandering in the school farm like an orphaned ghost. There was one teacher, nicknamed Potty, who kept a watchful eye over Malcolm and

nurtured his art work. While he was at boarding school Uncle Andrew rolled a tractor on himself and was crushed to death. No one told Malcolm for several months, so as not to upset him, and he found out one day at prep, by letter.

Most of his friendships at school were mute. He loved Ropati Vaii in the sixth form but his English was non-existent so they mostly said, 'Hey wait for me!' in the weekends, wandering round the empty school grounds. They both loved the Rolling Stones. Malcolm also fancied Ropati's younger brother. At Motukiore only he and his brother swam with togs on, as white boys. Some of the Maori boys Malcolm grew up with were truly amphibious, taking their clothes off at the smell of water. At boarding school they all had to shower together and for Malcolm it was erotic torture.

On Sunday afternoons they played scrag, a kind of rugby without rules, with up to 50 a side. One Sunday Malcolm was running with the ball and a boy called Julian Dashwood deliberately ran right into him. It was like being hit by a car and Malcolm glided through the air in a glorious flight before the ground rushed up and hit him in a second thump. At first his bones felt scattered and he lay there for a while recollecting himself. When he got up all he could see were the hills at the back of the school farm like a breaking green wave and he had the wonderful idea he could bound over them in seven-league boots. At that point his consciousness left his body and rose in a sort of spiral until he was looking down from about 100 feet in the air. It was quiet up there, and still, like a special effects video on pause and mute. From this hawk's-eye position he could see everything, including himself. His body was running around in a weird dither and the other boys were panicking. The next thing Malcolm remembers is being tenuously back in his body which was running away and he could hear someone giving chase. A pile of rocks appeared and his body started throwing them at the boy who was following and Malcolm was shouting at him. He was still only very faintly back in his body. It was all very disconnected, as if someone or something was covering and uncovering his eyes and ears and all other ports of entry. By now a hundred boys were chasing him; some were gaining and he ended up diving into a thorny snarl-up of blackberries on an island in the middle of a stream to hide from them. Eventually they spotted him and, laying planks over the thorns, came in and carried him out like a struggling trophy. He had been mauled by the blackberries and was covered in bleeding scratches and gashes. Nobody said anything; it was a kind of religious procession, but he knew he was now beyond the pale. After shining a torch into his eyes and declaring he wasn't concussed the school doctor referred Malcolm to someone he called 'a psychiatrist, if you like'.

His impatient parents drove him to Auckland to keep the appointment at the doctor's chambers. Malcolm took an instant dislike to the psychiatrist who looked unhealthy and waxen, like a mortician. The whole place reminded him of a presbytery, a home for renunciates whose relationship with the human body was occult, tainted, a place where minds were dissected, vital fluids drained, arteries truncated in a kind of joyless necrophilia performed for the sole purpose of perpetuating a race of bonsai. Malcolm's refusal to co-operate in any way with this ghoul offended him and another appointment was made for the next day with a different person, a male nurse who gave him a shot of 'something to relax you'. It was a truth-drug, probably sodium pentathol. Then the male nurse took him into a small room the colour of amnesia and started asking personal questions that were in Malcolm's view so improper he couldn't answer them. He had never had any kind of intoxicant before and as the drug took effect he began to describe what he wasn't going to say, and as his resolution not to tell got firmer he found he had to explain in ever greater detail what he had resolved to conceal. He had never talked to anyone about his personal life before but in that room, with the male nurse listening, Malcolm talked for an entire day. He has no idea what he said. For months afterwards he was exhausted and felt he had lost everything that made up his personality, all to no apparent purpose. He felt he had been raped. Things went downhill from there. He was diagnosed as 'slightly schizophrenic' and given a bottle of pills. He was supposed to take one every day but didn't. Every now and then, whenever he remembered, he took a handful just to keep the level in the bottle going down. Before he went to art school he decided to set fire to himself. First he poured petrol over all his drawings and the notebooks he valued so much and set them alight. As he watched them burning in the incinerator it was such a shock he couldn't go on.

Before the flight out of his body Malcolm already knew there were unmapped areas of the mind it was best not to tamper with. He remembers going to look for an old Maori cemetery in Okaru Gully that, although no one knew where it was, he had seen on an inch-to-a-mile map of the area represented by the symbol of crosses. There was an influenza epidemic in 1853 which wiped out an entire village. When he reached the bottom of the gully the air seemed to thin and he started getting increasingly hypersuggestive. He found a burnt banded rail's nest, the first he'd ever found, but there were no houses for miles so the origin of the fire that burnt it was mysterious. Then he saw some old peach trees in the scrub which corresponded to the site of the village. To get to them he had to go up into a grove of rewarewa, trees he always regarded as sinister because of their glossy, bottle-green foliage and serrated, *fin-de-siècle* leaves. The bush there was full of the strangling creepers supplejack and bush lawyer and there was no way of hurrying through. When he had threaded his way deep into the heart of the grove he realised he was surrounded by a flock of shining cuckoos. He couldn't see them but they were all singing loudly. Malcolm had only ever heard them singly before so it was alarming. The shining cuckoo can project its song. If it's singing and you slowly walk towards where the song is coming from it seems to jump to directly behind you so you can never be quite sure exactly where the bird is. Now there was a deafening, shifting choir of ventriloquist birds all around him. It was broad daylight and the unseen birds flitting from tree to tree struck him as the noise of the sun. He began to sense someone or something was following and warning him off and knew he had to get out of there as fast as he could. But he was caught up in the bush lawyer and supplejack; it was as if he had wandered into one of those nature films where the growth of plants is speeded up. The creeping vines seemed no longer to be creeping but swiftly weaving a web of nooses, snares and lassoes to hold him fast. The only way out was forward. After a space in time in which, while the vines moved swiftly, Malcolm struggled in a dream-like slow motion, he finally escaped from the clawing green hands and found himself wandering on cattle tracks in the manuka and rushes. As suddenly as they began the shining cuckoos stopped singing and now there was an ominous silence. There was no pattern to the tracks; the aimless cattle just milled about and followed each other. It was like being trapped inside the bovine mind. He kept coming to dead-ends and cul-de-sacs and was forced to go back towards whatever he was convinced was following him, fighting to contain a rising panic. He couldn't scream because if he heard the echo of his own scream bouncing back off the towering cliffs it would be a mocking of his entire being. So he kept going in a blind, frantic stumble until all at once he was in pasture on clear ground and was no longer being followed. As he lay on the grass flooded with relief he felt as if an old witch was putting a sign up behind him saying, 'Don't come looking again.'

The telling of this story sent Malcolm into a paroxysm of yawning and after a good night's sleep, he left the next morning to catch his bus up north. What he had told me was frightening and uncannily familiar and I suddenly remembered that once I had been in a bus driving slowly down Karangahape Road when, to my surprise, I saw myself walking along the street. *Looking good*, as they say, *going somewhere*. Then this other me, who didn't look in my direction, was swallowed up by the bustling Thursday night crowd and the bus I was in overtook me.

Malcolm's out-of-body experience begged the question whether he had ever fully come back into his body and his tale of calling the hawks reminded me of something Tobias once told me. Apparently the Asmat took their dead to a designated elevated place and left the body for vultures to pick the bones clean in a practice he called a 'sky burial'. Then when the representatives of the sky had eaten their fill and only the skeleton remained the people came back and retrieved the skull which was sometimes used as a pillow to sleep on.

My mind kept returning to the great vanished forest of kauri and I began to wonder about the history of trees and our insatiable need for them. Pre-European Maori destroyed half of the country's forests. Then my own Viking ancestors came in wooden boats and set to work like industrious termites on the first tree they met. When I closed my eyes I could see them like an absurd ditty in my head; behind their picket-fences, in their wooden houses, on their wooden chairs, at their wooden tables, with their nimble pens writing down versions of recent events on the wood-pulp-paper of trees, trees and more trees, with the tongues of burning branches warming them. Then like clockwork, once a week, out they came in unison to pray to their wooden God in their wooden churches on their human knees, for absolution. And as I looked closer with my accusing look, it seemed to bounce off them and turn on me like a bolt of lightning. In its flash I saw myself on my English elm, at my Irish pine, in my fake-wood unit writing my own side of the story and for a moment I couldn't catch my breath and felt literally petrified.

I read in a book I borrowed from the library that trees are the earth's oldest living inhabitants. Some are four thousand years old and must have held in their branches countless birds and even species long extinct and I wondered if these ancient trees remembered and if their outstretched arms ever ached for the touch or song of creatures long gone. As I sat in my own wooden ditty I read about the fragile plants that were transported here by sea in specially designed portable glass cabinets called Wardian cases, invented in 1836 by Nathaniel Bagshaw Ward. The sugar maple, Douglas fir, English oak, desert ash, and bat's-wing coral tree; the *pinus radiata*, cedar of Lebanon, gingko, elm, gorse, Formosan cherry and the flame tree; all these and many more were carried in ships to live in harmony or dissonance with the native flora. One book told of the attempts to introduce birds from the northern hemisphere to our own very different conditions. Possibly the most spectacular failure, at least in metaphorical terms, was the nightingale which was accustomed to migrating east to France in the English winter. After they brought it to New Zealand, come what it believed was winter the eloquent bird took off east as usual and died of exhaustion at sea, en route to Chile.

Dear Douglas,

I'm flattered by your attention, something I haven't received before. Perhaps you can put that in your book. Even at that age I was hanging onto reality by a thread. I was semi-detached even then. My only grounding was the boys I loved, Jimmy Te Hira at that time. I knew I should love Peter Karaka but he was almost too close.

My father jailed Peter's mum for beating up his little sister Huia. So there. The big philosophical questions for me were ethics, not land formation or birds. They were my retreat. I try not to whistle. Sometimes I do, then I come down with a thump. Peter and I had to sort out what happened in the long grass at the top of the road waiting for the rural delivery van. We didn't touch, but he forgave me for all my father's excesses. He'd just lost his mum, though I have a perfect picture of her as a severe woman perfectly capable of beating a baby. Huia walked stiffly as if every step hurt, which I'm sure it did. Peter would have known all that. From my parents' accounts he went bad and became a disappointment. I hated those assessments. I felt very inadequate.

Love, Malcolm

– 12 –

Invisible mending

It was after my return from New York in 1987 that Janet Frame first invited me to visit. At that time she was living in Levin. In the fifteen years since then Janet has moved house more times than I can remember. Even after what was to be the final move south, she shifted twice again. If asked she is very vague about her reasons; sometimes no reason is offered as if no reason is needed. She reminds me of the star witness in a never-ending criminal trial whose testimony is so valuable and damning she must be moved from refuge to refuge under complete protection. Sometimes I get the impression Janet herself is staying put and it is the houses that are moving. No matter where she lives, whenever I'm approaching one of her houses the surrounding area, as if by some gravitational pull, begins to resemble her fiction. Everything takes on an air of hyper-reality; the shops, the houses, the people, even the plants and flowers in the gardens all seem to wear inverted commas. I start to notice odd juxtapositions, the wheelchair shop next to the Chinese haberdashery, the Masonic Lodge next to the dairy, and especially in Dunedin, the people walking the streets all look like relatives of Janet's with their pale Scottish faces, wind-hectic cheeks, op-shop clothes and piercing stares. Often there will be someone standing on a corner with a visible infirmity. And the closer I get the more mysteriously ordinary and outrageously mundane the houses appear until I finally arrive at the most ordinary, the most mundane and by the aura of extreme stillness and silence I can always tell that Janet Clutha née Frame lives here. Janet is married to invisibility so to actually see her is like catching sight of one of the 'little people'; a fairy, an elf or gnome-ess. Even to write about her gives me the feeling I am picking a lock with a skeleton key she did or didn't give me. By the time I arrive at her door I feel like a hopeful character about to enter an unknown narrative.

I knock or ring, a child's patter, the sound of breathing and a key inserted. The door opens and she is standing behind a mesh screen, key in hand looking puzzled. Who? What? When? As she peers I say, 'Janet, it's me,' and then her smile ripples out to greet me. 'Oh Douglas, it's you. Yes that's right. Of course, how lovely to see you.' She speaks in little gasping breaths and somehow flirts with each word as it escapes her. Although barely above a whisper, her speech has the ringing clarity of a great diva who is resting her voice. Now the mesh door is flung open. 'Do come in.' She is shorter than me with her often described and now white blizzard of hair. Janet's body is a secret, well covered in baggy, brightly coloured floral prints and she moves continually, her gestural signature a kind of upwelling of mirth, punctuated by a slight regulatory tic. When excited she flaps and swings straight arms and takes tiny staccato steps; her movements are infectious and sometimes I join in. 'Go through.' She stands aside in the dark hallway and as I pass her we perform a complicated ritual in which she simultaneously avoids and graciously accepts a kiss. She closes the two doors and then locks us in.

'Tea, instant coffee? Oh thank you. How kind!' as I give her a gift of a book of poems and a diabetic muffin. Janet lives in a nest. There are boxes and papers and piles of things and many little clearings to sit in and behind screens, in the main room, enthroned, the computer. The house has blankets at some of the windows to muffle the noise and there are crocheted doilies on little tables, Afghans and tartan rugs on the couches and chairs. I feel I am inside a baggy handmade garment with all its tucks, seams, stitches and many folds showing. The other rooms are the sleeves, leggings, gloves, hat and gumboots to be worn when staying in. As she makes us a drink and I stare at things, trying to commit them to memory, we talk and catch up. 'Are you on somewhere?' she always asks. Sometimes I am. She strokes the word 'dancer' and it catches fire. We take our drinks and Janet chooses the space where we sit. Often we share our ailments; when I first told her about my condition we talked, glancingly, about death and she said, quoting, 'a terrible beauty is born.' Once I went on so much about my illness she said, in a pause, 'Can I tell you about mine now?' When she had trouble with her leg she told me, 'I can get it to work by persuading it to be faithful to the other one.' And then she tap-danced on the kitchen floor saying, 'They want to put a camera inside my knee but I'd rather tap-dance.' At first I didn't know what she was doing but then I could see she was dancing for me.

On some subjects she will not be drawn. Her work is out of bounds; once I asked her outright how her book was going and the way she said, 'Pleeeaaase don't ever ask me that again,' silenced me. But then sometimes she makes the faintest of innuendoes to the work she's doing and my ears prick up as if I heard a mermaid singing. The first time we met she sat in a chair like an oracle and when she spoke she kept interjecting the words 'she said' and 'so she said', referring to herself in the thirdest of persons. Afterwards when I tried to tell people what 'she said' I could hear her saying those very words and I wondered if she knew she had put a lock on the contents. I am always nervous before visiting Janet but once we get started we flow from one topic to another in what she once called 'meander-chats'. After we have eaten and drunk and gathered up the crumbs she says, 'Would you like to see Penny now?' and then takes me through to a room full of brown cardboard boxes with a grumpy black and white cat sitting in one of them, staring at us. 'She's angry at the moment,' Janet murmurs. Penny Panty-hose is the scaredest cat I've ever met; sometimes she rushes into the room and when she catches sight of me she gives me such a look, as if she's searching through a microscope for any way to get rid of me. I suppose it's hard for Penny to constantly change her address. We then go back and sit in a different clearing in the main room in front of a giant turned-off television. Janet loves to marvel so I bring her little tidbits; I tell her about Giacommetti's struggle with smallness and thinness, or Rumi's meeting with Shams of Tabriz, or I read her a letter from Emily Dickinson and we get to marvel together. When Janet listens it's like she's holding a buttercup under my chin to catch the colours. She makes tiny noises of encouragement, surprise and congratulation and I always feel this gift of utter attention can only be given by someone who has, at some time, been utterly ignored. On the odd occasion Janet is upset about something she takes on a bewildered, beleaguered, doom-laden air and then all is rusty and grim. She tolerates my attempts to comfort her because 'we're in the same boat'. The first time I met Janet I thought she looked like a female Orpheus who had managed by some miracle of invisible mending to knit back together the torn-aparts of her and had come back singing. All the trickster, questing heroes that come to mind are men. Janet has to be Shakespeare's or Maui's or Loki's sister; gnome-ess or castrated Orpheus. The tricksteress.

To conclude we make a tour of the garden. Doors are unlocked, I am let through, doors are locked again. The pepper tree, the pineapple mint, the shrivelled leaves of an unsprayed fruit tree, the clothesline, an old crippled chair. In Shannon she had a pet sheep and one day it got through a hole in the fence and into a paddock where there was a whole flock of sheep and Janet stood staring at the flock for a long time trying to work out which one was hers. I can't remember if she finally recognised her sheep or not. And then I leave.

In Levin she offers to walk me to the bus station but when we get outside it looks like rain and I say, 'No. don't worry,' and she says, 'Are you sure?' as if I am giving her a treat. Her last words are 'Now, you are not a stranger,' and she stands like a post as I embrace her. I start walking away and when I look back for a final glimpse I see Janet running as fast as she can, back inside.

On one of his visits to New Zealand to see me Tobias and I took the Newmans bus to Shannon to visit Janet. They hadn't seen each other for several years and when he hobbled off the bus with his walking stick the waiting Janet murmured something sphinx-like about the passing of time. That afternoon, in her old farmhouse by the river, I felt as if Janet and Tobias were my ancestors, from a dream-branch of the family. They were the 'housekeepers of ancient springtime' and I was their mokopuna.

I half-expected to meet a buffalo in the hallway.

– 13 –

Dead dreams

After my previously detailed experiences in New York, my return and breakdown, I could feel a family of dances welling up inside me, waiting to be born. But first I needed to regroup and decided for some strange reason to have a holiday in London – not the ideal place to convalesce. But I had friends there and once or twice spent an English Christmas with them. London, for me, was quaint and chilly, with log fires in cosy rooms, English people measuring accents, Antipodeans talking about home, and an incinerated partridge in a pear tree. On the way I stopped off for a few days in Sydney to visit some friends. By then I had been sober for three months but one night I found myself standing outside a pub rooted to the spot, trying with all my might to resist the temptation to drink. I stood there for at least half an hour, immobile, perfectly balanced between the forces of craving and abstinence; it was evening and the sun went down on me. I seem to remember at one point a seagull mistaking me for a statue; it came and perched on my shoulder for a rest before flying off again. When I finally succumbed and went in they told me they'd just closed. Back at my friends' house nobody was home so I drank everything I could lay my hands on, including the dregs of a bottle of liqueur that tasted of melted sweetened cockroaches, with a sting.

I was fragile when I arrived in London in mid-1988 and intended to stay only a month or so. Just enough time to complain to everybody I knew about my terrible experience with Limbs and to soak up their sympathy along with the alcohol I was now regularly drinking again. One day in the tube I ran into Lloyd Newson, an expatriate Australian I knew, who once danced in New Zealand but had been living and working in London for years. I had heard rumours about DV8 Physical Theatre, his new company, and was curious. We started talking and stood there for a long time catching up. He had seen me on television dancing in a film of *Last Look*, one of Paul's dark pieces, and said I'd be perfect for his next project. When I told him about my nervous breakdown his eyes lit up and he said that was even more perfect. The work was to be based on the gay mass-murderer Dennis Nilsen, exploring desire, the search for love and the creation of monsters through alienation. Lloyd is a compelling person, pale, with an acne-pitted face and an arresting gaze. That day, in the Underground, he was wearing a cap to protect the shiny egg of his shaved head and his eyes shone as he zeroed in. Despite my reservations I agreed to meet again and at least consider his offer.

Over the next week or two Lloyd wooed me assiduously. He told me about the new way of working he was developing which involved delving into one's own experiences, sharing them with the group in structured talkfests and then improvising. The work was devised by the whole group with Lloyd as director. Lloyd was a revolutionary and his passionate disdain for the polite world of dance was music to my ears. I read the book *Killing for Company* based on Nilsen and watched videos of DV8. Lloyd said all he could offer me was risk. He has a degree in psychology. After meeting Nigel, his collaborator and one-time lover, and Russell whom he was wooing at the same time, I decided to do the project.

We rehearsed in a small space in the East End, going to and fro on the tube. The process was laborious and confronting but I had no problem sharing my secrets. In a way it was a relief. Everything said in the room was strictly confidential and once we began to move the improvisations were videotaped. I discovered I wanted to blindfold sexy Russell, pull his pants down to hobble him, and lie on the floor and put his booted foot on my face. When Lloyd asked me to quiver all over as I moved into a foetal position, I felt like a scrap of paper shrivelling up as it burnt. Nigel was the most enthusiastic, constantly pushing himself and us to go further, dig deeper, *hurt hurter*. He was the colour of milk with auburn pubes and moved like a nude spider monkey with a strange pathology. I was required to strangle him then play with his dead body as if it was a floppy doll, just as Nilsen had done with his victims, whose bodies he kept under the floorboards and in the fridge. Nigel was the corpse *par excellence* and after I killed and toyed with him, I put him in a bath and lay down beside it. When he came back to life in a vengeful resurrection he slithered out of the bathtub and over me. I can still taste his sweat and feel his hot breath as I lay still, feigning death in the house of horrors.

I remember standing in the middle of the rehearsal room crying while Lloyd kept asking questions, trying to get me to 'go deeper', saying, 'No, don't sit down, just stay there and tell us how it feels. How does it feel?' Lloyd challenged and questioned everything. He was omnivorous, a messianic nosey-parker, driven by a deep sense of anger and injustice that I identified with. He could also be kind. I remember him saying that whenever he was on the street and approached a group of straight men he found himself subtly changing the way he walked so as not to appear effeminate. That was me too. Lloyd's shaved head was both daunting and vulnerable. His skull bulged in odd places, like the helmet of an extraterrestrial. The back part of it seemed to contain a coiled-up reptile that on occasion woke and spat fire from his eyes.

The finished work, *Dead Dreams of Monochrome Men*, was brutal, grim and disturbing. The critics raved and audiences were paralysed with admiration. We toured Britain and then on to Avignon. After one performance in the provinces we were heading back to London; the others took the train and I decided to drive back in the truck with the crew. At the time I was staying in Lloyd's flat in Camden and when I arrived I was stinking, weeping drunk. There seems to be a frozen river of grief inside me and copious amounts of alcohol thaws it to a flood. Lloyd listened kindly to my outpourings and then, in the morning, he and his frighteningly efficient flatmate frog-marched me and my hangover around Camden Market, adamantly refusing to let me cringe in my bedroom. I think Lloyd was surprised at the length and breadth of my lamentations and had a quiet word with the crew about letting me get so intoxicated. As if they or anyone else could have stopped me. I had warned him I was in no fit state to have my emotions dissected, but we both took the risk. In some ways I was probably the ideal person to be incarnating murderous alienation on stage each night. I rather enjoyed it. After our last performance at the ICA in London we lit sparklers in the dressing-room to celebrate and accidentally set off the fire alarm. The whole building was evacuated and we stood outside with the audience in the cold, waiting for the fire engines, trying to look puzzled.

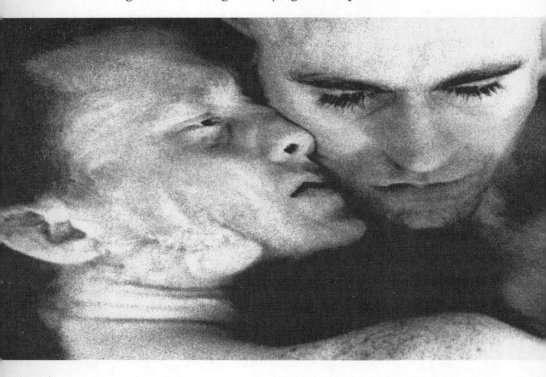

The next year I returned and an award-winning film was made of *Dead Dreams*, as we called it. It was a draining work to perform; one had to live it and though the world of dance festivals was clamouring for us we all felt it was too difficult. I think it was that work which made DV8's enviable reputation. Lloyd hated dance as opposed to physical theatre and although he gave me valuable tools with which to continue my own work, for years afterwards, whenever I created pure dance I could feel his disapproval. It was like having another version of my father in my head. In 1992 my own company toured to Britain and the Netherlands with *Gloria*, a work I made after my HIV diagnosis and experience of bliss at the meditation retreat. After opening night in London I went out to dinner with Lloyd and Wendy, his sidekick, and two friends, Ann and Mark. Nobody mentioned the performance and when Mark, who was deeply entrenched in the dance-world they despised, said anything, Wendy repeated it in a nasty little voice half under her breath. While this was going on Lloyd squeezed my knee under the table in sympathy and it dawned on me that in bringing a Taylor-influenced work of celebration to cool, angsty London I had irrevocably blundered.

When I think of London now I think of the Underground and the escalators like assembly lines ferrying battalions of ill-looking people up and down, always full, with a narrow gap on the right so those in a hurry can. They all looked recently departed and I thought of the ones going up as the saved and the ones going down as the damned. Seemingly unmoved by either fate, the commuters all wore the same blank expressions. There had recently been a fatal fire at one of the stations and it still smelt of smoke and fear. In the trains we elaborately ignored each other. It was a different indifference from the New York brand, less hostile, more bitchy. I remember one day being in a half-empty train when a group of bizarrely elongated people got on. They were obviously a family and were all very tall, thin and horsy. They looked like human giraffes and as they draped themselves around the carriage, taking two seats each, talking to each other in a haw-hawing English I could barely make out, I thought, here comes trouble. I half expected the other occupants of the carriage to ridicule them or at least flash one of the dirty looks they had handy but then something unexpected happened. People began to seem to doff their caps and tug invisible forelocks as the burbling family nodded in greeting and I realised they were aristocrats; getting on the tube was a lark for them, they were slumming and everybody glowed in a gala of condescension.

The place I felt most at home in London was the Egyptian Room at the British Museum. I loved the black marble sculpture of the hawk-headed Horus and another of a goddess shaped like a large woman with the head of a hippopotamus and the feet and hands of a lion. There were mummies of baby crocodiles and people dead and bandaged for thousands of years with all the things they needed placed in their tombs with them. It seemed almost cosy.

– 14 –

Hatching and Seacliff

I was on my way to Tuakau driving deserted country roads through lush green paddocks when I saw two children walking hand in hand on their way home from school. A little boy and a little girl, just a glimpse, perfect in every detail, they must have been only five or six. They looked like those photographs you see of children who have gone missing and after a long search are eventually found dead and interfered with, confirming all the worst fears. As I said it was just a glimpse but they looked so impossibly innocent I had a strong urge to stop the car and go back and warn them. The only thing that stopped me was the even stronger feeling that if I did I would somehow be implicated in what I knew was about to happen to them.

My first memory is of being held up high, dangled over a pool of muddy water at the Auckland Zoo and seeing a hippopotamus rise up and open wide its jaws. I watched transfixed as a whole cabbage was thrown in, and as the monster snapped shut its jaws and disappeared back into the water, I began to scream.

But there is another first memory, so faint it's almost an intuition. I was pressing my forehead up against the cold glass of our lounge window watching a lady in a long white gown on the verandah of the house opposite. She was dancing back and forth, her white dress fluttering like the wings of a moth. The memory is dreamlike, soundless – just the moth lady fluttering back and forth in my mind.

One day my sister Christine and I were playing grown-ups with an old disconnected telephone when one of us reached up to plug the frayed wires into an empty electric socket and then switched it on. The wall blossomed into a long golden flame and we shrivelled back in twittering fear. That was long before we went to school, when we stayed at home with our mother who did outwork for a sewing factory, taking short breaks to save our lives. In my parents' bedroom was an old industrial sewing machine where Mum sat for hours with

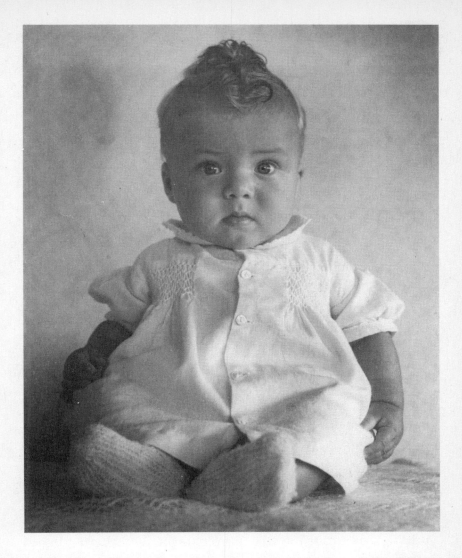

her foot on the pedal, as if she was in a car driving somewhere, slowing down for the fussy bits and the corners, then going faster and faster straight ahead. On the wall of their bedroom was a framed colour photograph of a young Queen Elizabeth II. The Queen looked just like my mother and when I was little I got them confused and thought that somehow my mother had been the Queen but now for some reason wasn't. One reminder of her former power was her green fingers; everything she touched burst almost immediately into flower. Our house was surrounded by roses, snapdragons, pansies, jasmine and night-blooming hibiscus and inside Mum grew ferns, a creeping hoya and elephant's ears. She also taught me how to knit and I knitted myself a blue jumper, very slowly and proudly, mistaking the astonished comments of our neighbours and family and the silence of my father for admiration. In our house my father reigned supreme and Mum was his slave. She cooked and cleaned and sewed and tried to take care of everything, but what she did was never enough. There were four, then five of us, and sometimes in exasperation a thin, high-pitched voice came out of her that jabbed like a needle straight into me. 'Just wait,' she said. 'Just wait till your father gets home.' And so we waited. And waited. My father was a 'lineman for the County' and after work he liked to go to the pub. Hidden behind frosted glass windows he and his cobbers drank oceans of beer and talked about footy until the tide went out. At first closing time was at 6 p.m. but then they changed it to 10, as if now we were bigger we had to wait longer for him. He was quick-tempered and sometimes got into fights, boasting to us when he got home. 'I showed them,' he said, and, 'That showed them.' It was usually Maoris he showed. When he was home my father was always 'growling', as he called it. Almost every night after we went to bed they argued, with Mum's needle voice jabbing at his growling rumble. They went on and on, her voice getting thinner while his got thicker. Or there was the silent treatment. Once she found a long black hair in the car. No one in our family had long black hair. That hair was like a tightrope, a line drawn in the sand, or the lit fuse of a bomb. It was evidence. As far as I know he never hit my mother, only us, rarely, when we deserved it, but the feeling that came from him was so charged with violent frustration the air was thick with it. Tiny red pitchforks of anger shot out of his blue eyes and into what or whoever he looked at.

My father was also something of a daredevil. Once at the Wellington Zoo he reached through the bars of a cage to shake hands with the gorilla. The gorilla politely took his hand while Dad winked and beamed at us. After pumping the great ape's arm in a parody of greeting, Dad's cocky smile changed as he realised the gorilla wanted to get to know him better. In fact it was gently pulling my father closer to the cage. A small crowd buzzing with excitement gathered as Dad attempted unsuccessfully to free himself. Time stood still and added its gaze to the amazing sight of this indefinitely prolonged handshake. It was a kind of demonstration of the wonders of evolution. After what seemed like years the zookeeper came and made the gorilla let go of my ashen father by banging on the cage and yelling. 'You could have lost an arm,' he said in a tone of disappointment.

So it wasn't all bad, we went on lots of trips. We drove around the South Island, stood on a glacier and cheered as the speedometer in our Vauxhall turned over into a row of zeroes.

When I was little my friend was Pana Williams. He lived across the road from us in an old wooden house buried in a forest of trees. It was dark in his house and an old Maori lady with something wrong with her gave me Maori bread to eat. Outside under a vine-mountain Pana showed me colour photos of ladies with no clothes on. They had black hair like spiders down there. We wrestled and he reached inside my pants and squeezed my thing so hard it hurt. But I still liked him.

I went to Harrisville Road Primary, about a quarter of a mile up the road from our place. School was hard and boring until I learnt how to decipher the signposts of the letters of the alphabet, to read and write words, and go where they were pointing. Books were journeys I was always taking, starting with Jack and Jill, Hans Christian Andersen, on to Tarzan, the Brothers Grimm, and beyond. I have a strong relationship with some words. At school once we were given penpals of the same age from another school; when they read the names out mine was Bruce and I started crying, I don't know why but I hated the name Bruce: the 'B' seemed so bossy.

At first at playtime and lunchtime I sat with a big fat Maori girl, a medium English girl, and a silent, skinny Indian boy. We talked about where babies come from. The Maori girl had toes that were on a slant from the big toe to the little one and I liked the way her feet looked; my toes were straight across, so I tried to squash them up to look like hers. We played knucklebones and I learnt to skip with the girls. The other kids started teasing me – and then there was my dancing.

From the earliest time I can remember I was always dancing. I still don't know what possessed me; perhaps the fluttering white moth laid its eggs in me and my dancing was a kind of hatching. In Tuakau, South Auckland, in the early 1960s a dancing boy was frowned on with a frown handed down for generations. Dad, a former halfback for Counties, said to my mother as I wafted past, 'Christ Pat, get him out of my sight!' and I responded by dancing wherever and whenever I could. Now, in the school playground, at playtime and lunchtime, I improvised wild, expressive dances in full view. And after school in our backyard with only Mum as a witness as she did the dishes in the kitchen, I continued. Though I never looked at anyone when I was dancing, I could feel their eyes on me. Only my mother's eyes felt safe. Mostly the gazes were uncomfortable, as if I was covered in a hot, itchy and spreading rash. But I was caught in a kind of hurricane and nothing could stop me from responding. By some mysterious, unspoken agreement my public displays were never referred to. No teacher or student ever mentioned what I did. Instead names were attached to me; I was a SISSY SKITING, and when I heard those words it was as if my body was getting smaller and smaller, hotter and hotter with the shame and anger of it so that dancing became a way of not disappearing or burning up entirely.

Eventually from on high I started to hear the word 'gymnastics' and this word was gradually inserted between me and my unmentionable writhings. I took the bait and became obsessed with doing the splits, walking on my hands and the aerial cartwheels called baranis. When we went down the main street of Tuakau, Mum pushed the pram with my youngest sister in it, my other sister who is two years older rode on the back and I walked on my hands beside them.

After a year or so of lessons at the Pukekohe Gym Club it was decided I had 'potential' and I was invited to train at the Leys Institute in Ponsonby, Auckland. My new coach, Warren Burroughs, invited me to stay at his house every weekend with his wife Lyn and their two small children. They made me a part of their family and their place in Grey Lynn was like a second home. They were both retired gymnasts and now trained champions. I wanted to be a champion too.

In the long walks to and from the bus station I discovered that the city, which was like a giant graveyard with its deserted grey mausoleums and occasional lost-looking mourner, was haunted. I kept seeing the same 'weirdos', as I called them, in the same places, acting strangely; talking to themselves or drinking out of brown paper bags. One colourfully dressed woman with electrocuted hair directed traffic at Three Lamps, warning drivers of impending accidents in a loud, authoritative voice. Another stick-thin man in a threadbare suit walked very fast, leaning back at a peculiar angle like a pair of out-of-control scissors, stopping at regular intervals to gesticulate with a wild precision. But on Sundays Ponsonby Road was full of Polynesian families or 'Islanders' as they were most politely known, on their way to and from church. They seemed huge to me; the women in long, baggy, brightly coloured dresses with hats like tropical flowers and the men, formal on top with shirts and ties, but from the waist down in what looked to me like old grass mats. They seemed so happy, so at ease in their roomy bodies; always in groups, pools of warm, rhyming humanity punctuated by the lonely, jagged, white weirdos.

One day as I was walking down Ponsonby Road towards the bus station a man came from behind a fence and said, 'Hello, son.' He asked if I knew any nightclubs round here. I had seen one on my travels called the Galaxy so I mentioned that to him casually, as if at eleven years of age I was a regular. Then he asked me where I was going and when I said the bus terminal he replied that was a coincidence, he was going there too and would I like a lift in a taxi? And I said, 'Okay, thanks.' Then he hesitated a little, as if just remembering something. 'I just have to get some money from my room. I live just in here, come in for a minute while I get it.' I don't know why I went into the dingy boarding house with him but I did. The man looked a bit like my father but he was run-down, like his room, and had some front teeth missing. There was a couch decomposing against a wall the colour of a bruise. Once I sat on it I was politely, almost apologetically, molested. I can still feel the way he looked at me just before he touched me, his eyes like breath on my skin, and then his fetid mouth tried to suck out from the depths of me a fluid that didn't yet exist. Up until then sex was a mystery but now I knew what some people did; a veil lifted and I noticed other men hanging around the public toilets at the bus station and I could see the intricate, almost invisible mating dance they were performing. This dance includes sly glances alternating with direct looks, tiny movements and gestures of the head, eyes and hands, and ritualistic pacings with meaningful pauses up and down in front of the chosen one. They were like spies with coded signals or some kind of human chameleon that had developed ingenious methods of camouflage to outwit its vigilant predator. All the movements needed to be carefully chosen so they could be turned into natural gestures at any moment; such as when a policeman happened to be passing, or if you misjudged your mark and found yourself propositioning an uncomprehending, possibly violent (though always innocent) bystander. I joined in this secret ritual when I was about 12 and found it took some extraordinarily detailed choreography to convince my adult victims I wasn't police 'bait' before they consented to abuse me. Sometimes we did things in the toilet cubicles. The men's toilets at the bus station seemed to be carved out of solid rock in an underground cave with moss of a poisonous green growing in nooks and crannies and water constantly trickling down walls covered in rude words and drawings. Or they took me to their empty houses or flats, usually in a taxi. Often they were young and hand-some and to me their erect penises were so big I could hardly believe it. Once I drank stout in bed with a bald-headed man old enough to be my grandfather while we watched rugby on TV. I hate rugby.

This was how I found out what I was and that it was so disgusting it had to live where other people went to shit. And I instinctively knew my dancing had been a giveaway clue. Now it made me cringe to think of what I used to do and I trained myself to pretend that 'I' was someone else.

I was also training long and hard at gym, learning how to work, discovering I had a natural gift. We all worked together, we were a team at Ley's, and the older guys took me under their wing, not suspecting my hidden interest in them. When I had to get up in front of the judges and the audience at competitions it was like the knife-edged void I had danced in at primary school but now the eyes watching were authorised. All of my fear and excitement seemed to sharpen to a point, making my body an arrow aimed at the air and the target of eyes that were now, literally, judging. I began to win gold medals and stand modestly on the top of little steps numbered 1, 2 and 3 to have the medals hung round my neck. Dad began to be proud of me, calling me 'champ'; even, to my shame, wearing my medals to the pub to show his mates.

At home, whenever I wasn't practising gymnastics I read books, lying on my bed with my pug-dog Toby curled at the other end looking at me blissfully. I was given Toby on my fifth birthday and we were inseparable. One day in the Pukekohe Library I found a book

by Janet Frame called *Snowman, Snowman, fables and fantasies* and fell in love. There was one story in particular, 'The Terrible Screaming', that thrilled me to the core. The last sentence read, 'Silence had found its voice.' I knew the terrible screaming she was describing, it was inside me, and I knew the Silence. I devoured that book and over the next few years, all the others by her I could find. Janet was my first hero. I hoarded scraps of information about her, astonished she actually lived in the same country as me. There was a photograph of Janet on the back cover of one of her books; in it she was standing in front of a kind of latticed wall, suggestive of bars or a confessional, looking with her frizzy hair and concentrated gaze like an imprisoned mystic. To me, one of her eyes looked kind and smiling, the other like the hawk in her first story, unsentimental and all-seeing. I looked at her face in the photograph often, shading one eye then the other, then neither. Silence had found its voice.

Remembering the beginning of my preoccupation with Janet makes me think of a visit Malcolm and I made to the ruins of Seacliff, the Victorian-era lunatic asylum, the day after our sighting of the trapped hawk. Seacliff was where Janet Frame had been taken in 1945. It is about an hour's drive from Dunedin, up the coast. Earlier that day we drove to Oamaru, the town even further up the coast where Janet grew up. It was raining heavily there so we followed by car a detailed map of something called 'Janet Frame's Oamaru'. This included a long walk. All we saw of that were the signs. And we couldn't seem to locate any of the buildings on the map. We kept getting lost. Then we had a fight about map-reading and ended up staring at an empty paddock with a vague depression in it that we thought might possibly be the site of Janet's now demolished childhood home. So I was determined to retrace our route to Seacliff to get my Janet-fix.

When we arrived the whole area was shrouded in a very poetic white sea-mist. I stopped the car and when we got out I noticed approvingly that the mist was drifting almost imperceptibly, and as it moved it hid then revealed then hid again the surrounding landscape. Green hills, with the occasional white house nestling in ink-black trees, sailed in and out of view as if they were being slowly towed past us. It was a mesmerising spectacle, almost too appropriately Gothic-revival, and I photographed it from about four different angles. We couldn't even see the Pacific Ocean but could hear it in the distance obligingly dragging its chains. The asylum itself was off the main road and up a hill. It had long since been closed and the main building demolished and through a line of closely planted poplars we could see an unpromising huddle of buildings. At the large, closed gate there was a little sign that said, thrillingly, 'Entry by appointment only.' I wondered how we could get an appointment at such short notice and walked up and down outside taking photos and trying to look natural as Malcolm took photos of me until I summoned the nerve to open the gate and go in. It looked like an old farm with large stone outbuildings and the toppled remnants of a castle. At what I thought must be the office I rang the bell and a youngish, smiling Heathcliff lookalike appeared. Yes, the building was open to the public and he would give us a tour. We took the short $20 tour and asked if it would be possible just to wander round the place on our own. Although he readily agreed he followed us anyway, at first at a slight distance and then gradually he caught up and began a running commentary. We learned that he lived there and was slowly trying to do the place up, to turn it into a tourist attraction. But 'business' had been slow and we gathered his wife had just left him. His hobby was restoring old sports cars and here and there in the ruins were gleaming vehicles crouching in various states of disrepair under tarpaulins. I was having misgivings about even being in the place and knew I could never tell Janet I had been here. 'This was the kitchen,' he said. 'This was where they worked.' 'This was where they ate,' but I wasn't listening. I was imagining tourists flocking to Seacliff to visit a Janet Frame theme park. The mind boggled. I could almost see it. The Janet Frame Experience: 'Lie where she lay – experience, without pain, a simulation, correct in every detail, including the gag, of the electric-shock therapy she herself experienced. We have professionals trained to give you the once-in-a-lifetime, life-changing experience yourself, in a stunning replica of the hell-like ward she was actually in, of being told you are about to be given a lobotomy! And for just an extra $25 we are now in a position to offer you our deluxe package which includes the Reprieve, in which you get to lie, in authentic period costume, in a hospital bed holding a first edition of *The Lagoon and other stories*, the book that saved her life ...'

I came out of my delirious reverie as we reached an area that made the hairs on the back of my neck stand authentically on end. A warren of brick and stone buildings stood around a large courtyard. There was a two-storey edifice of white-washed brick with a doorless doorway opening immediately onto a hallway completely taken up by a warped and crooked staircase that seemed to go nowhere. The stairs began at the very edge of the doorframe, so that if there had been a door it would have had to open out. It looked like a mouth with far too many teeth. I took a photograph. Adjacent to this was another building with another opening that looked as if it had never had a door. Inside two white china toilets squatted ('Sit where she sat!'), like the abandoned thrones of a race of troglodytes, one for the King and one for the Queen, right next to each other. I took another photograph. The last structure in this area was off to the side, an afterthought. It was wooden, painted white and cream, and looked like a row of stalls for the royal horses. Our guide was saying in hushed tones, '... and this is where they were kept.' In each cell the walls had recently been painted in high-gloss cream. At a certain angle, when the light fell on its ridges, you could see that the entire surface was carved with interlocking words, signs and marks made by the beings kept as punishment in solitary confinement here. I took at least three photographs of these cries for help. As we were leaving, as an added extra, because he could see we were connoisseurs, the smiling man took us into a little room and with glowing eyes showed us various contraptions, articles of clothing, torture, an elderly wheelchair, even a strangely formal letter from one of the inmates to the outside world. The last thing we saw as we staggered out was the rust-coloured morgue, in a copse of trees, in the shape of a Russian dacha, with its empty slabs and marble floor that sloped to an ominous central drain. In the ante-room there was another wooden staircase that had been ripped out of a demolished building and put here for storage I suppose. It was leaning against the wall, as if slightly out of breath, looking very calculated, even stagy, like a discarded set-piece from a film adaptation of a horror story by Edgar Allan Poe, 'The Stairs That Dripped Blood'.

As we drove away in a stunned silence I couldn't help wondering how my photos would come out.

One day when I was twelve Toby wasn't waiting as usual at the school bus-stop for me and our little red car was there instead. I knew before I even saw the look on Mum's face he had been run over and killed. He had been so utterly innocent and trusting that sometimes I had been overpowered with a desire to hurt him. This was so bewildering, I felt in some way guilty of his death and for years afterwards I had a Toby-shaped absence as my faithful companion. It was only very recently that I turned around to find his absence had disappeared.

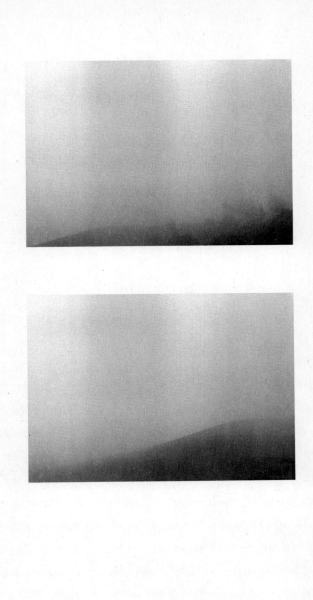

– 15 –

Broken fall

My mother still says, 'You went to high school when you were twelve,' as evidence of how advanced I was. The proper age was thirteen. At twelve I was more advanced than she could possibly have imagined and schoolwork held no interest for me. In class at Pukekohe High I surreptitiously drew stick-figures in my exercise books, one on the outside edge of each page, so that when I flicked quickly through I could see the figure moving in impossible gravity-defying routines. It was something to do. And my disguise was working; I had a girlfriend, Trish, and nobody seemed to suspect me of being a 'queer'. The endless jokes we made about this aberration centred on the word 'latent'. Anything unusual said or done by a boy provoked a chorus of, 'God you're latent.' The first person to spot the deviation was then accorded the honour of the most masculinity, at least until the next infringement.

My best friend at high school was Rick. He had brown hair, glasses and was as thin as a whippet. His family was richer than mine and when they were out we'd lounge around drinking his father's whisky listening to 'Indiana Wants Me' and Janis Joplin. Once we tried to light each other's farts and when his caught fire in a tail of flame we ran round the house screaming blue murder. One night when I was staying at his place I couldn't help myself and with my heart thudding a warning, I made the first move and seduced him. We were both very offhand about what happened and never mentioned the fact that whenever we could we kept doing it. But our friendship was charged with new meaning and we began to act like tiffing lovers. We often went to the beach in his father's car and Rick's driving was erratic and made me nervous. The wheels on my side were always slipping off the tarseal into the gravel, sometimes sending the car into a spin. My nagging criticism seemed to make his driving worse; gears graunched, we bunny-hopped and skidded and stalled and argued violently. One day when he dropped me off I was so angry that to have the last word, I left the passenger door wide open then stalked inside, knowing he'd have to reach over awkwardly and shut it before he could screech off. After that when we had sex it was more and more like being in the badly driven car; shuddering, swerving abruptly, misjudging distances so our teeth and bodies clashed painfully. Rick's glasses steamed up and if he took them off his eyes were stripped naked, like blind moles dragged blinking into the light and physically, I went off him. This was the beginning of a pattern. I only wanted what I couldn't have. But it was all a secret within a secret and I never told Rick about my other adventures at the bus station.

In the fifth form a boy who was almost an albino arrived at our school from Canada. Kelly had white eyelashes and pink skin. His parents were hippies and soon we were the coolest group in school, smoking dope and getting pissed off our faces. We were the in-crowd and decided it was time to go to a real nightclub in Auckland. I felt desperately uncool as we descended the two flights of stairs to the entrance of the Tabla nightclub in Lorne Street one Saturday night, where to our surprise the guardian at the door, a dwarf with long blond hair, barely glanced up at us before uttering the magic words, 'Two dollars each.' The long, low-ceilinged room throbbed with live, extremely loud rock music. We found a table inches away from the dance floor, emptied our smuggled Bacardi into a jug of iced Coke and settled in. Occasionally a stray beam of light meant for the dancers shot its dislocated arm out and over us, then jerked back to the dance floor. Following the spasmodic path of light I noticed a shape in the opposite corner. It was a girl, tiny, with long black hair half-covered with a scarf. She sat alone, in a peculiar position, with her back slouched over and her head down as if looking at the floor, but not as if she was relaxed, rather with all the tension of something cornered, frightened. She was dressed in an ingenious combination of fringed shawls and draped veil-like garments, with rings on the toes of her bare feet and hundreds of bangles glinting like armour on her wrists and arms. While I was staring at her the band had been on a break, then suddenly the music started up again and I watched this strange girl as she began to move her body to the music, at first almost imperceptibly, as if taking tiny sips. She was still sitting bent over, her bare feet picking up the rhythm and sending it up through her body in a wave, and as the rhythm deepened she was rocking and jerking back and forth on the bench in a kind of ecstatic foetal position, her head nodding mechanically like a puppet's. Then she got up and began slowly again, all by herself in the corner, seemingly oblivious, still bent over but more supple, looking at first as if she was toying with the music, finding a way in. Then gradually, by degrees, the music seemed to enter her body, to possess her, increasing the pressure until she was a storm of flying arms, legs, hair and clothing, dancing with such concentrated, manic intensity that people began to whisper and point. I was dumbfounded. Who was she? Was she mad? How did she live in the world? What was her name? And how did she move like that?

After that first night I went to the Tabla as often as I could; the strange, magical girl was usually there, always alone, supremely unapproachable, burrowing into the eye of the music. She had different disguises; sometimes she was a bikie chick with chains, a mute swagger and boots, at others she wore a red dot between her brows, but mostly she was the gypsy urchin and I named her Rachael and gradually, instinctively, began to imitate the way she moved and dressed.

The summer of 1972 I was 16 years old. I took my first LSD trip with Rick and Trish at the Rolling Stones concert at Western Springs, and although all I remember of Mick Jagger was a giant mouth and lips on top of a sinuous, floating scarf on top of a bulging crotch, jabberwockying across the stage, that day I discovered the existence of other worlds as surely as if Martians had landed in the main street of Tuakau. Or it was more as if the drug itself was a space rocket and I was taken to another planet that resembled everyday reality in the same way a scientific description of the sexual act resembles a shattering orgasm. As soon as I could I found a job in Auckland, left school, and moved into an old house in Franklin Road, Ponsonby with Trish, Rick and the other members of our gang who were ready for lift-off.

I liked Trish; she was blonde, bovine, with a slight lisp and a whimsical charm, but I never really desired her and even though we went through the motions our bodies both knew my heart wasn't in it. But now we were hippies so everything was cool, far-out and laid-back; most of us had girlfriends (the term for them was, strangely, 'my old lady', or 'your old lady'), and both sexes went barefoot, wore Indian muslin and love beads and smelled of patchouli. Despite our hatred of the square world of our parents, the 'old ladies' did most of the housework and homosexuality was unmentionable. During the day I was a clerk in what was then called the Social Welfare Department, the government agency that now suckles me, but at night and on the weekends I moved in other dimensions. We took acid trips together in those first glory days and the old house in Franklin Road became a creaking galleon riding the night sky, through the ragged clouds, past the shooting stars, onto the dark side of the moon. We were pirates of inner oceans, revelling in our booty and we were intensely free, the world was ours, until it wasn't and we weren't.

My job was in a high-rise building in the centre of the city and it mostly consisted of writing the name *E.C. Puddick* at the bottom of official letters to clients of the Social Welfare Department. *E.C. Puddick, E.C. Puddick, E.C. Puddick* until my hand ached. I was beginning to feel like a robot when one morning, as I was walking from my bus-stop to work I spied a familiar shape in a passing bus. It was Rachael on a Number 10 from Onehunga. The bus turned into Victoria Street, stopped and she got off. She was still dressed like a creature from another time and place and walked rapidly with her singular hybrid of jerkiness and fluidity. There was a spring in her gait, a power held back, as if she could leap buildings if she chose. Daylight only added to her mystery; she was as thin as a boy, geisha-white, with a red bud of a mouth I couldn't imagine ever uttering a syllable. Although her clothing was outlandish she never struck a false note; Rachael was always native to the Timbuktu of her imagining. Her black-rimmed eyes darted from side to side, scenting danger, and as she flew up Queen Street I fell in behind her. Just past the Town Hall with its clock hands showing an emphatic eight, she disappeared into a barred doorway with the sign *Moller's Art Gallery*. I knew it would be a mistake to approach her directly. What could I say? 'I like your clothes'? So instead I waited every morning at the appointed hour on the appointed corner and followed in her wake, like a stalker or a mourner, and continued to see her each Friday night, from a distance with my friends, at the Tabla or a new nightclub, Levi's Saloon. I approached her only once, at Levi's. I asked her to dance with me. She was sitting alone at a small table and looked up with total incomprehension, as if I had spoken in Swahili, and although I repeated the question, she made no reply.

There were complications; the new nightclub we all went to was across the road from the bus-station where I still sometimes picked up men. It made me uncomfortable, as if I had two maps of Auckland in my head; one I shared with my friends, and the other secret map, and when they started to intersect I could hear warning bells. After Trish found me in bed with a Maori boy I took up with another girl who, believing I was madly in love with Rachael, did her best to imitate this manic gopi in the hope of getting my attention. To no avail. I wasn't in love with Rachael, I simply wanted to be her. Sometimes, with my own Rachaelisms as a kind of camouflage, I managed to give paranoia the slip, dancing myself into a state of such bliss that the music and I swapped places. But not for long. After being caught yet again in bed with a boy by my now thoroughly confused girlfriend I vowed never to inflict myself on a female ever again and became a homosexual at last. *One of them.*

My first job was short-lived. I was fired for wearing an earring, and in the same way as I went through a series of jobs – clerk, shop assistant in a boutique for men, then in a music store, clothes-presser, kitchenhand, then a petty criminal – so I went through new looks, new friends, new flats and new drugs, taking everything right to the edge and beyond in my search for the elusive in-crowd. Each drug had its own little community and matching ambience derived from its effects. It was like being an actor in a series of scenes from a movie that would never end. Some scenes were edgy, amphetamine, with jump-cuts, knives and abrupt, nasty endings; others were pre-Raphaelite dream sequences with grass and hashish, soft-focus dissolves and slow fades. Acid was special effects, surrealist, the day of the triffids, all split-screen paranoia and subtitled hidden meanings. Then came downers with orgies of swooning camera angles and glammed-up bambis choking on their own vomit. Heroin was the last stop, it was film-noir, with blackmail, murder and disdainful beauties stiffening in the terminal chic of rigor mortis. Every scene seemed to require at least one death, a blood-sacrifice, and we played our parts in deadly earnest. Even the deaths seemed unreal, it was all hush-hush and stories of high-speed corpse drop-offs at the door of Accident and Emergency before screeching back for the next instalment. Rick trailed me through the whole production, except for heroin. Sometimes I lost him for a while but he invariably turned up, engine revving, when it was time to move on, saying my name and grinning like an idiot. I was always relieved to see him.

The soundtrack for these films had its own drug logic: Pink Floyd, the Rolling Stones, David Bowie, Roxy Music, early Split Enz, Lou Reed and Patti Smith. We were kamikaze, tatterdemalion, tireless in our pursuit of the highest high and the *innest in*. Each scene had a presiding deity, someone so saturated with that particular drug they were its personification: Adrienne. Sally. Tilly. Natasha the vicious. Whip-wielding, pearl-strung Chrissie, and Denise. These drug-stars were famous for the amount they could take and still stay upright and they wandered the streets like saints in samadhi protected from harm by devotees, their jewelled feet not quite touching the ground. And if they got so high they overdosed it was an apotheosis and they immediately ascended to their rightful place in our pantheon. Sometimes the different scenes accidentally overlapped or collided. The spectacle of someone on speed talking compulsively to someone nodding off on heroin was amusing, but when a person in the grips of an LSD-induced psychosis was caught up in a high-heeled herd staggering around on barbiturates the outcome was more unpredictable. I seemed to be required by some megalomaniac *auteur* to act out every role in every combination imaginable and it took years. After one 'heavy scene' on LSD I lost my tenuous connection with reality and found myself climbing the walls of a room that was bucking and rocking like a ship in a cataclysm. Rick was there. I was drowning in fear and he and another friend tried to calm me but they couldn't hear the announcer on the radio giving detailed descriptions of my loathsome condition and they couldn't see the repeating loop in which a car kept driving up and delivering to the door a hooded apparition who was coming to collect me but then vanished as the

177

car drove up with her in it again. They made me drink some rusty water and wouldn't take me to the hospital though I begged them to and somewhere in the middle of this nightmare a hamster-like person sidled in and sat next to me. He asked me questions in a soothing voice, looked at me with sparkling eyes and then sidled out again. In the following days and weeks as I emerged from what was then called a 'bummer' I was grateful my friends had not taken me to the hospital because if they had I would almost certainly have ended up in Oakley, Carrington, the bin. Acid psychosis was quite common in those days when the drug was so pure and there were stories of people who had freaked out and were still in the bin, rotting under a blanket of sedatives.

Then one day the hamster-like man with sparkling eyes came to visit. He was dapper, dressed in a white tailored suit, still sidling but with a suggestive impudent air, as if he had a fascinating secret. His name was Billie Farnell and I learnt he was a famous eccentric, a notorious piano-playing homosexual who collected oriental antiques, china dolls, Maltese terriers and malfunctioning boys. He must have been in his early forties then but to me, at 17, he was old. He wore make-up and drove a red MG sports car. The second time he came to visit he brought me roses. We went out in his car together and people gaped as we drove past. Billie was an impulsive driver; if he saw a flower or a statue he liked in someone's garden he just stopped dead in the middle of the road to point it out. He wore huge cameo rings and golden sovereigns, a fob watch, a sporty tweed cap and always had silk handkerchiefs frothing from his jacket pocket. He took me to his home in Bell Road, Remuera. From the street the house was completely hidden by trees and we entered through a pagoda-like gate and almost crawled on our hands and knees down an overgrown path as the sound and smell of dogs rushed up to meet us. The house itself was smothered in creepers; one vine in particular seemed to be squeezing it like a hungry boa constrictor. Billie opened the French doors with the flourish of a magician. Behind a beaded curtain the rooms were crammed with antique furniture, as if the contents of several strange houses had been emptied into one, and everything was, as Billie liked to say 'sinister and oriental', with the vomited-up black lava of Chinese cabinets and dragon-thrones trapping a tribe of porcelain dolls in its coils, their dead glass eyes staring with looks of astonished innocence into space. Billie whispered, 'Do you like the antiques?' in a melodramatic voice as he danced on ahead of me, leading the way. My reflection floated past in clouds of gilt-edged mirrors hung next to tapestries embroidered with wisteria, unravelling birds and the same silky white fowls that wandered freely through the house, pecking at the pattern on the Persian carpets. Everywhere I looked something bizarre and precious appeared, as if the furniture and objects were multiplying before my very eyes and would keep on mutating until they burst the skin of the house.

'I'm a collector,' Billie breathed. 'It's a disease.'

In the kitchen, behind another beaded curtain, was a mess; unwashed dishes, junk piled on top of dying furniture with a miniature, manic dog like a wind-up toy running back and forth on an ironing board, faster and faster, barking at us. It had long white hair, like Franz Liszt.

'Eccentric,' Billie whispered as he yanked me back into the lounge. It was overwhelming and claustrophobic. You had to squeeze past things to get through and move piles of photo albums, magazines and slack-jawed puppets to find somewhere to sit, and once you sat down the claws of a mummified cat dabbled in your hair.

In the aftermath of my most recent disaster I needed what is now called a 'positive role model' and Billie was it. He made me laugh. I began to see the funny side; Billie was an expert at the funny side and told shriek-fuelled stories so exaggerated and labyrinthine you had to believe him. He played the piano for me, sitting bolt upright like a child at one of his several baby grands, his heavily ringed fingers dancing over the keys, playing Gershwin and 'Kitten on the Keys'. His playing was like everything else about him, with as many flourishes and decorative curlicues as humanly possible squeezed in the gaps between the notes. The embellishments ran dazzling rings around the melody, threatening to overwhelm it, and there would be a sense of mounting urgency before Billie, glancing proudly at me, let the melody emerge triumphant. A photograph of his dead mother Edith sat on the lid of the piano in front of him and as he played it was as if he was reading the music from the lines of her face.

We sat and pored over his photo albums as he explained his bizarre and wonderful life to me. I enjoyed his company and the dinners we

had together and one night when he asked me to stay I immediately agreed. So I lived with Billie on and off for the next five years while I continued my headlong journey. Under his tutelage I started my own collection of Chinese antiques, had a white suit made, and changed my surname to something hyphenated. I was Bosie to his Oscar Wilde. He introduced me to Fellini.

There were other boys that hung around. He called them his 'lame ducks'. One boy had, as Billie explained, 'something wrong in the plumbing department', his 'bum had never been joined up' and after several unsuccessful operations had to make do with a colostomy bag. Another had parents who had hit him constantly about the head with bits of four-by-two. He was diagnosed as mentally ill, 'quick to anger and dangerous'. He studied judo, was in contact with beings from another planet and could see ghosts. There were schizophrenic boys, boys who were arsonists and boys with what Billie called 'hang-ups'. I was the chosen one and watched as the others clustered round him as if he was the mother duck. All the while Billie talked on the telephone and made cups of tea.

He was an old-school homo with an exaggerated horror of female anatomy. One night, as a test, I followed him around the house chanting, 'Labia, vulva, womb, clitoris, cunt, vagina,' as he ran from room to room begging for mercy. He ended up locked in the bath-room dry-retching as I continued my recitation through the keyhole.

Billie did have women friends but to be acceptable they needed to be either eccentric, or voracious collectors of Chinese antiques. He took me to visit Flora McKenzie, the notorious madam, at her brothel in Ring Terrace, Herne Bay. She was an old woman, overweight, in a floral house-dress, sitting on a Chinese throne with a glass of whisky-and-milk in her hand and her coffin propped up beside her. She sized me up: 'I see you in blue underpants with diamonds in your ears,' she said, wiping at her milk moustache. Billie told me that when his pet monkey Mowgli met its gory death (which is another story) Flora requested the simian's testicles which she then had made into a pair of earrings to wear at the next of her many court appearances. She grew strange succulents that hung in rows from the ceiling; long pale-green ropes called donkey's tails or *sedum morganium*. They grow from a cutting and Flora gave me one which is now an elder with its own descendants.

Somewhere along the way gymnastics fell by the wayside like a shed skin, my father disowned me, my parents finally separated after the owner of the long black hair was identified as his Maori mistress, and one of my sisters got caught in the sick, glamorous world of prostitution and heroin I ended up in. The last time I saw Rick was at a nightclub in Melbourne, just before he found religion and got married. He was drunk, spouting gibberish, full of the same old manic intensity, stalling, restarting and jumping at you, then falling over laughing like a fiend. I introduced him to my friends as, 'Rick, he's insane.'

I kept moving out of Billie's then having to be rescued by him before moving back in. And Billie was infinitely understanding the next time I moved out again. He called me 'naughty' and sometimes 'very naughty'. At 17 I spent two weeks on remand in the slimy entrails of the stone fortress of Mount Eden prison for using a prescription poison. The police discovered a friend and me tottering very carefully on the white line in the middle of the road in the early hours of the morning, hitch-hiking. When I got to a certain point of intoxication I had black-outs and did things I couldn't remember. There was something inside me so wild it was almost murderous. For a while I lived with some prostitutes and a pretty Australian thief called Steve. He and I hung around together, scrounging heroin and shoplifting. He was a light-fingered virtuoso in a leather jacket and I was his decoy. We swapped what we stole for drugs. I lusted after him and he worked it, sprawling in front of me with his legs wide open, a sexy sneer on his face. He injected me slowly, sliding the needle into my vein like a considerate lover, staring into my eyes as he pushed the plunger in, smirking as the drug orgasmed through my body. But he wouldn't let me touch him. He was straight. When one of the girls noticed how much I wanted him she said, 'I wouldn't worry about it if I was you. His dick's so small you're not missing out on anything.'

At around this time I was at a nightclub when I saw a girl who looked vaguely familiar. I kept staring, trying to place her, then realised it was Rachael. I hadn't seen her for years. She was heavier, dressed normally and her burning aura had gone. I went up to her – she was no longer unapproachable – and started a conversation. She was friendly and confirmed that yes, she was Rachael, her real name was Judi-Ann. Judi-Ann told me she'd been in a mental hospital having shock treatment because, 'I couldn't go round Auckland thinking I was a gypsy for the rest of my life.' She said she was happier now and gave me her phone number but I threw it away. I wanted the old Rachael, who would never have spoken to me or even have had a telephone.

One night at Billie's I had an unforgettable dream. Although I dreamt it over 25 years ago it's clearer to me now than what I did yesterday. In the dream I was living in a foreign country, in another time, in a white marble temple set on an empty expanse under a cloudless blue sky. I was a student, one of a group of about ten other boys, all of different races. Somehow I knew we were in training for an event that, though unstated, was the purpose of our existence. We lived in silence, ate special foods, slept on mats on marble benches and spent every day practising precise dance-like movements. Our teacher was a tall, distant figure in a white robe with long black hair and eyes like emerald fishes. He was kindly but exacting, and he required perfection. Despite a strong feeling of discipline there was no fear or coercion in the dream, all was happy, peaceful and intensely focused. We practised in a courtyard in front of our teacher. There was a fountain of crystal clear water leaping behind him, the blue sky and the hot sun overhead. When the day we had been training for arrived we woke breathing adrenalin, we had no idea what was going to happen but knew we were ready. At a signal from our teacher we began our movements as usual but this time he urged us to go faster and faster until we were dancing a dance we hadn't been taught; leaping, spinning and flinging our bodies like ecstatic dervishes. There was no music. Then the teacher, who always moved with a weighty deliberation, pointed his finger at a cinnamon-coloured boy in the front row, who ran towards him in slow motion and with a mighty effort leapt in the air, speeding up and spinning like a top until he was a cork-screwing blur which then disappeared completely with a sound like the crack of a whip. At exactly the same moment as the boy disappeared half of the teacher's face also vanished and then one by one, at his signal, we all ran towards him, hurling our bodies into the air like suicidal, criss-crossing angels, each disappearing with the crack of a whip, causing another geometric section of the teacher to be erased until only his pointing arm was left hanging, like the fragment of an exploded statue in the air and then, with the last boy, that too disappeared. Although I was gone, in the dream I could still see the empty courtyard in the empty temple on the empty plain with the fountain still splashing and the sky still cloudless. That was in some ways the most powerful part of the dream, how I could be absent and present at the same time. It was almost as if I was seeing the deserted temple from the sun's perspective.

I was proud of my ability to dream such a special dream and told it to anyone who'd listen, trying to fathom its hidden meaning.

When I was about 19 I took a few ballet classes but stopped going when the teacher kept asking me to take off the long sleeved tee-shirt I wore to cover the storm-coloured bruises and needle-marks on my arms. Finally, or so it seemed at the time, I found myself in a small room in a massage parlour in Sydney lying naked on my back, stoned on heroin, smoking a cigarette, idly watching in the mirrored ceiling above as a fat, hairy, middle-aged Greek man laboured on top of me. As I watched we became one composite angel-monster, a kind of human scorpion stinging itself to death and for a split second I was terrified this nightmare insect would scuttle down the wall and touch me. I was twenty-one. Soon after that I overdosed on smack and when I had recovered enough to get on a plane, flew home to New Zealand almost totally consumed with fear and despair.

At first I stayed with Billie. He was always there to pick up the pieces. On my birthday he gave me a book of photographs of Vaslav Nijinsky, the legendary, doomed dancer and choreographer, telling me, 'He looks like you, so pretty!' But now there was little he could do for me. I sat on his couch night after night while he was at work, getting high, listening to Patti Smith, staring into space. Sometimes I pretended to be one of his dolls.

Mum had a new boyfriend called Bill and when I first met him in our old house in Tuakau she stood slightly behind him like a sign-language interpreter, gesturing desperately for me to stop as I regaled him with all my latest doings in full. But Bill, who we thought with his bald head, mutton-chop sideburns and glasses wasn't good enough for our mother, beamed benignly as I told him what he was getting himself into. Bill was brought up on a farm, like Mum, and was extraordinarily informed on a wide variety of topics. When he gave us the benefit of his knowledge in depth, Mum took up her original position slightly behind him and nodded off, with a lingering smile of admiration on her lips. One day in the car with her, my younger brother and I took the opportunity to list Bill's faults in extensive detail. Mum listened silently and when we'd finished said,

'Oh, well, at least he treats me decently.' And so he did, and still does. At the time I think I was jealous my mother had a boyfriend and I didn't.

Then one evening I was with a friend who was on her way to look at a room for rent in Whitaker Place. At first I was going to wait in the car but at the last moment decided to go in. The door of this old, spooky two-storeyed white house was opened by Malcolm. In a sort of foyer sitting on a chair was a life-sized, life-like wax sculpture of a naked man, like the congealed ghost of waiting. Malcolm led us into a room then disappeared without a word to make a cup of tea. The room was high-ceilinged and the walls were papered in newsprint, roughly painted white so you could still see the cancelled words swarming underneath. It was empty except for three chairs, a plain wooden table and a trio of white papier-mâché models of the Egyptian sphinx, on wheels. Malcolm had made them; he was a sculptor and painter, the *enfant terrible* of his year at Elam, former student and drinking companion of Colin McCahon. Though I plied him with questions he wouldn't look me in the eye as he talked and laughed behind a cigarette-clenching hand. But he was beautiful, with fine features and soft sparrow-coloured hair, and when our eyes finally met they locked with an almost audible click. It was one of those moments often described as 'love at first sight' but although I had a premonition we belonged together it was more like the feeling you get when you've been trying to recall a word or a name for days or even years and although it's on the tip of your tongue you just can't get it. Then when you've forgotten all about it, out of nowhere you suddenly remember. When I first met Malcolm it was like that sudden remembrance.

On our first night out we went to a gay bar and got drunk. I distinctly remember Malcolm asking about my family history and as I talked he kept slipping in disparaging references to his own. Then we went back to his place and fell onto his single hospital bed. After that first night I moved in. We made love constantly, as if we were the two halves of a perfect whole separated by some grisly accident and fucking was the only way of sewing the torn flesh and amputated bone together again. Malcolm's grey, fluffy cat Tammy sat and watched us with a look of outrage. Although she obviously disapproved she was like one of those self-appointed guardians of public morals who, for the sake of the community, constantly watch pornography. When an arc of flying come splatted on her fur she was so disgusted she moved a little closer. Malcolm's white skin was so translucent the branching veins of green and blue were like rivers running through a pale landscape, with only the thinnest of membranes stopping them from flooding. In between bouts we told each other things that had happened to us but mostly Malcolm asked questions about my torrid past and I answered him. From the little he said I gathered he had been on the same drug merry-go-round as me, only nine years ahead, and was the third person convicted for possession of LSD in New Zealand. Speed had been his drug of choice, and he hinted at gruesome hallucinations and a brief committal to a mental institution. Despite all this, he graduated with first-class honours – his 1971 thesis is legendary – and was so beautiful he had been pursued by a bevy of admirers of both sexes. One woman was psychotic and still stalked him; she turned up one night screaming abuse and festooned the garden with used tampons and several hundred thousand Italian lira when we wouldn't let her in.

Malcolm was secretive. He had files and folders full of his tiny, spidery handwriting with titles like 'Downhill' in barely perceptible

pencil on the outside and it was forbidden for me to even ask about them. Every now and then, when he was out, I held my breath and sneaked a look and once caught a glimpse of a sentence as it scuttled back to its hiding place. It said, 'O the longevity of socks.' During the day he was a storeman in a grain-store but in the evenings and on the weekends he was always painting pictures of naked, skinny boys that looked like a younger, half-Maori him or making bizarre,

punning gadgets. There was a door handle at the top of a pole, and a small wooden chair covered in hundreds of things: egg-beaters, junk jewellery, old rusty keys, cutlery, a baby's dummy. No sooner had these marvellous objects come to life than they disappeared, to be replaced by the next in a seemingly endless litany of irony. In his studio he transformed the bay window into a miniature stage, with no entrances or exits. It was hung with plush velvet curtains and papered with pages from the telephone book. To one side was mounted an old hand-basin which took on an eerie, inexplicable presence, as if it was about to speak. The house was a few doors down from Elam, the art school from which he graduated, and when I asked him why he didn't exhibit his work, he prevaricated. He told me McCahon had warned him against exhibiting but that didn't ring true as a good enough reason to sacrifice a career. Malcolm had an almost fanatical aversion to the art world and seemed to be engaged in a silent and deadly battle with a host of enemies, many of them former suitors. The years of amphetamine abuse helped create his isolation and I was terrified of becoming someone he fell out with. I noticed that for Malcolm people were either 'really lovely' or 'shits' and the progression from the former to the latter was often alarmingly swift, with some exceptions. He had unanswerable stories of the shabby things people had done to him and, quaking in my boots, I had to agree that yes, people were shits. But when Malcolm saw how crestfallen I was the first time he got angry with me he relented and after that I was largely exempt from his harshest judgements. We collaborated in creating an alter ego for me – someone who was lovable but completely selfish, charmingly poetic and illogical, but messy and demanding. I was grateful for the identity, so close to the truth, and my new character was allowed to get away with things I couldn't, because his life had been 'twagic'.

Compared to Malcolm's constant industry my lack of direction was painfully obvious. He encouraged me in all my wild ideas, trying to get me to focus on one, asking the question that I believe saved me from the abyss of drugs: 'Is there anything in your life you ever really wanted to do?' I had to think for a while; nobody had ever asked me that question; it seemed outrageous, and then I remembered how I'd always loved to dance.

And in one of those coincidences that make life feel like a fiction it turned out his previous boyfriend had been a dancer in a new dance company called Limbs. Their studios were close, in Grafton Road, so, at the age of 21, I began going several times a week to classes in ballet and modern dance technique while Malcolm supported me.

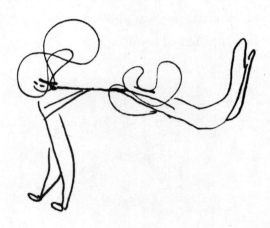

Part Three

– 16 –

The eunuch experience

As I trained to become a dancer, the photographs of Nijinsky in the book Billie gave me were a kind of sustenance. I considered it more than a coincidence I had seen the book in the window of Whitcombe and Tombs the day before Billie bought it. The photographs exuded a weird charisma intensified by the resemblance between the Russian dancer and me. Nijinsky created and inhabited a world I recognised and the look on his face was come-hither. I felt I could almost step into the photographs, put on his body, and go for it. When an old drug-friend I met on the street said, 'You look just like one of those old photographs of Nijinsky as a student,' I knew my dancing must be improving.

After about six months of classes with Kilda Northcott and

Mary-Jane O'Reilly, both members of Limbs, I was pronounced ready to go to their ballet teacher. Dorothea Ashbridge was a dancer in the Royal Ballet in London for twenty years. Originally from South Africa, she married a fellow dancer who was a New Zealander and when their dancing careers ended they came to New Zealand to teach and direct. Dorothea had a formidable reputation; stories of her strictness floated through the dance world like pollen. 'Going to Dorothea' was a bit like going to the dentist to the uninitiated and when the other students heard the news they looked at me with a mixture of sympathy, envy and awe. One evening, in a state of terror, I climbed the stairs to her studio in Karangahape Road to find a small, elegant woman in her forties, dressed entirely in pink, sitting in a haze of cigarette smoke at the piano, curling her eyelashes. She looked me up and down and said, 'We'll see,' and after that first class declared that perhaps she could do something with me, so I began going every morning to her advanced technique classes. The French names of the exercises disguised a subtle and sophisticated torture and my feral muscles fought back. We did pliés and tendus, battement and frappés to scratchy records of Chopin and Mozart as the windows misted up and Dorothea patrolled like an imperious figurine. She was merciless and exacting but knew unerringly when to encourage, when to criticise, and when just to leave a withering look on the offending body part. There were one or two girls in the class who had learned ballet since they were little and they could do things. As the exercises at the barre got faster their feet moved so quickly they were like birds' wings beating time to the music, arriving and leaving perfect positions with an astronomical punctuality. Their slippered feet seemed to be on speaking, even punning terms with the floor and while the bottom half of their bodies performed wonders, their arms, necks and heads were unconcerned, regal, with a smile that denied any strain or difficulty. There was another girl with a ghastly, frantic smile. She was like a nun, toiling gratefully in a puddle of sweat for years, always smiling, never complaining. But her feet were unresponsive pink trotters and no matter how hard she tried she never improved. There was not a dancing bone in her body and she laboured like someone in a nightmare fairytale, trying to spin a roomful of straw into gold, or empty the sea with a thimble. She stunk of desperation and we avoided her and made jokes behind her back. I think one of the girls gave her a stick of deodorant one day as a hint. But no one ever questioned her right to be there, to keep trying to propitiate the cruel mirror.

I felt I'd been accepted into a select society with its own language and rules. For me the daily repetitions were the skeleton of a structure that was a godsend. After years of being lost it was a relief to be given a map of positions that showed me exactly where I was. There was a definite front, side and back and moving from one position to another was like cutting geometric shapes out of the air. The counts of the music were the *when* to the *where*. Ballet is the art of kings, a colonisation of the body which then gives an elegant demonstration of the conquest of time, space and gravity, or death. Balanchine told a story about Louis XIV who was walking down a flight of stairs to his supposedly waiting carriage. When the carriage arrived at the appointed spot at precisely the same time as the King, he was very upset. When asked why, he said, 'You were *nearly* late.' I, too, was nearly late. As I became serious about dancing I heard whispers: 'What a pity,' they said, 'he started late. He'll be so disappointed. He tries so hard.' That did it. Every night, after a hot bath, I put my body on the rack, trying to lengthen the tight bunches

197

of muscles. Using pieces of furniture as wedges and weights I assumed the desired positions. Breathing prayers and muttering curses I stretched to breaking point a body I was determined to transform from mongrel to thoroughbred. Malcolm made a barre for me to practise on and, cigarette in mouth, he took my legs, one at a time, while I held on, and gently pushed them as high as they could go, in all the directions, front, side and back saying, 'This is boring.'

Although I became a contemporary dancer I always studied ballet technique. As it turned out it was good luck I started late; by the time I began my body was already too formed to be completely subservient to any technique. So once I'd learnt what I could from Dorothea, Paul and others there was still a part of me that was untamed and, when coaxed, it spoke its own body-pidgin. I stopped dancing at the turn of the century and now it has been three years since I took class. By my calculations, when added together, all my daily classes in 21 years of dancing come to approximately one solid year, day and night, without stopping, of practising technique and now, in my mind's eye, it is as if that year is rewinding. I can see myself doing all those classes again, but in reverse. Slowly at first, then faster, unlearning the body's catechism. Darting, swerving and leaping in schools of backward-dancing flesh, wave on wave of dancers migrating tail-first back to the egg, drawn in and out of half-remembered studios in New York, London, Madrid, Los Angeles, Chicago, Sydney, Wellington, Auckland, stopping to peck at the music and drink up the pools of our own sweat, with my classmates and teachers gradually changing though always repeating the same patterns, myself the only other constant. I can see faces I had forgotten and scrawls of movement like signatures being sucked back into the pen, and Dorothea taking back into herself the web of praise and correction, running backwards between lines like a striding compass with legs of steel, measuring our disappearance, until I am gone and Dorothea is the student in a class with a fleeting Margot Fonteyn and a lunging Nureyev and faces seen in books now being erased, then the video rewinds so fast it's a whirring blur which gradually descends like a plane reversing its take-off and as it slows down I see a class dancing backwards with someone in it I recognise and then, in freeze frame, not coming or going, Nijinsky, just hanging in the air.

Up there, in the moment of absolute rest, all is silence and the peace that surpasseth understanding.

In New York I was taken one evening to meet the composer Virgil Thomson for dessert in his apartment at the Chelsea Hotel. The dining room was Matisse-red with sumptuous old paintings of giant peaches, grapes and other swollen fruit and Virgil, at the head of the table like an overfed potentate. He was in his nineties, completely bald, fat, and hard of hearing. His eyes glimmered through plush chinks. I see him with an ear-trumpet but it was more as if his crackling voice was coming from the old brass horn of a gramophone. Somebody told him I jumped as high as Nijinsky and Virgil said he had seen Nijinsky dance in St Louis when he was a boy and it was not how high he jumped but how softly he landed that was so astounding. 'Do you land softly?' he asked. That I couldn't say, I hadn't landed yet, but he took a shine to me and we flirted before his nervous amanuensis shooed me away. I don't remember what we ate.

Nijinsky went mad in 1917 and spent the rest of his life in a state of catatonia. His celebrated leg muscles turned to flab and he never spoke, vegetating in institutions before dying in 1950. When I look at the photographs of him now it is the quality of transformation that strikes me. He seems to change not only costumes and positions but even his own shape as if he was subject to a series of possessions. Most uncanny are the half-human, half-animal, even half-floral beings. Bird of fire, spirit of the rose, panther, faun, he incarnated

metaphysical links in an unknown evolution and when he was unable, for whatever reason, to continue his open house he became an empty hovel. His last public performance he described as his marriage with God. Before he closed down he wrote his harrowing diaries and signed them 'God and Nijinsky'. Diaghilev, his lover and impresario, was apparently so germ-phobic he would only kiss his Vaslav through a silken handkerchief.

My budding career was the baby Malcolm and I had. I was completely happy as my new dancing body took its first steps. One night when we were giggling and tickling in a side room the shared front door slammed and someone ran upstairs. Brent, a sullen red-head, lived up there and when we heard a bang and gagging noises we laughed as if we were overhearing someone drunk vomiting. The next morning Malcolm went off to work and when I woke again the house was crawling with police. They wouldn't tell me what had happened but when they carried out a sheeted body on a stretcher I knew Brent had hanged himself. I ran outside and fluttered around the house like a fantail after insects. I couldn't bring myself to go back in. The house was malignant. I had to call Malcolm to come home. So we moved to a flat in Karangahape Road which was stifling, then to half a house in Prospect Terrace in Mount Eden. When he heard I was studying to be a dancer Mr Soma, our new Indian landlord, did a little dance for us and said we'd come to the right place because the grass there had 'acrobatic texture'. Somehow, after the first move, Tammy, our moral guardian, went missing and we soon acquired a tortoiseshell kitten who tiptoed down the hall, mewing. I named her Istina, after a character in a Janet Frame novel and later found out the word means 'truth' in Serbo-Croatian. The name

suited our Istina, who was a great truth-teller.

Those were halcyon days; we had a snug nest on the waves. With Malcolm as my inspiration I dived into art history, reading everything I could and gazing my way, through the reproductions, into the paintings and sculptures. One night, so he tells me, I ran into his workroom to announce, 'I want to be in the Renaissance!' Sometimes I read books aloud to him as he whittled and painted. Janet Frame's *Daughter Buffalo* was one. I wrote shamefully derivative poems, made a mosaic, and dreamt up dances I never believed would be made. Malcolm was fastidiously encouraging of all my endeavours, though he never hesitated to point out any plagiarism. As I continued my daily dance classes, for a while I had a part-time job at a gay sauna, the Victoria Spa. I let the men in, flirted with them, took their money, gave them a towel and a locker key, and later swabbed down the spermy plastic-covered pallets in the cubicles and the upstairs orgy room. Sometimes when I was doing the cleaning in empty rooms usually wall to wall with tangled, thobbing fronds of flesh, I practised my glissades and entrechats and pas de bourrée. When Malcolm, who was never a client of the sauna, came to pick me up after work on Friday night, he felt like a criminal ringing the bell outside while the people waiting at the bus-stop looked at him knowingly.

We were still living in Prospect Terrace when, after two years' training, I finally became a 'Limb'. My first major role was as a unicorn in Menotti's opera *The Unicorn, the Gorgon, and the Manticore* and on rent day Mr Soma surprised me by asking how I had enjoyed *The Eunuch Experience*.

Limbs were famous, sleek and sexy. Before I joined the company I went to their shows which were mostly short, snappy numbers to pop songs, jazz, even Jimi Hendrix. The works were humorous, accessible and relentlessly heterosexual, with occasional attempts at the serious, and the jam-packed audience screamed for more. Their concerts and image were the perfect concept, visual sound-bites of dancing flesh. Limbs were pioneering, dance as accessory, cornering a market no one else knew existed. They created an audience then shortened its attention. They were a kind of cult, eating bean sprouts, practising yoga and an obscure mental hygiene. And Limbs had a rock-solid centre. Kilda was 'gravity's angel'. She danced in the same way the *Mona Lisa* smiles – calm, inscrutable, seeing nothing, seeing everything – and when she moved you couldn't take your eyes off her. I hadn't really wanted to be in Limbs. They never seemed that interested in me and I was seduced by ballet but when they finally asked me to join, two weeks before I was to leave for the Australian Ballet School, I couldn't resist being famous. For the next two years I danced and toured in the company. I was eager to try my hand at choreography and after my first year Mary-Jane gave me the oppor- tuinity. There was already a dance waiting like a fist inside me. Those first efforts were largely forgettable. But, at that time, in that place, they worked, held together by a 'life-dealing want'. Most of the choreography was done by M. J., as we called her, the artistic director, or Chris Jannides, the founder and co-director of Limbs, who left after philosophical differences the same week I joined.

We danced in school halls and cavernous theatres, on makeshift stages at rock festivals and tiny platforms in shopping malls. We went to Australia, Japan, Papua New Guinea, the USA and Kohukohu. In New Guinea, in an outside performance, when Adrian lifted Debbie into a spread-eagled position on top of him, the audience of hundreds of semi-retired head-hunters in traditional costume

exploded. Pitch-black men in bird-of-paradise feathered head-
dresses, penis gourds and elaborately painted faces threw themselves

onto the ground in fits of hilarity. They were so excited, for a moment I thought they might attack us.

In rehearsals, whenever there was a break I joined Kilda and Debbie on the sidelines in the never-ending penitence of stretching. Kilda told me she had been hit on the head when she was little and now she was instinctual. Debbie, who was small, dark and prey to injury, was constantly searching for the special liniment, vitamin or exercise that would alleviate the pain she was in. We both wanted to be like Kilda and the first dance I made that is still breathing was *Knee Dance*, a 1982 trio for Kilda, Debbie and me. We loved it. It was our dance wedding.

After I left Limbs, Kilda went off to Sydney and I didn't see her for years, but in a strange way I did feel somehow married to Debbie. Our dance-lives were intertwined and she was my creature. When she stayed with me in New York, she wore a crumpled white chemise

I bought her in Paris, and took my mountains of empty beer cans to the store for the refund, which she then used to buy basics. She had curious fads and obsessions. I remember her placing a tissue on the floor then picking it up with her toes, moving it out to the side and back as if her foot was waving it, then letting it drop to the ground. Then she would pick it up again and repeat the process. This ankle-strengthening exercise was done something like 50 times while we carried on a conversation. Then there was the other foot. There was nothing sexual between us; she had a series of dark, slippery boyfriends in search of themselves.

In New York in 1987 I made a duet for Debbie and me called *Hey Paris*, based on a Brassai photograph of two men at a fancy-dress ball. One wears the trousers and the other the jacket of a single suit. Debbie is exquisite, and danced like a gazelle. In those days she was watchful, bright-eyed, as if something had frightened her into a porcelain submission. She seemed to be holding herself in readiness for the inevitable, with a brittle smile always at hand to wear while she worked out her options. I exploited her radiant fear and often Debbie was the one who ran to the top of a human staircase, or was dropped, sobbing, from a great height, to be caught in the nick of time. For such a little thing she had an incredibly loud scream. Sometimes it came out by accident and people would look at her in amazement as glass shattered. The pain she was constantly fighting turned out to be spinal degeneration and two prolapsed discs and, at first, no doctor or specialist took the trouble to listen. Even when she could hardly walk it took all of her tenacity to get anyone to take her seriously, but when they finally did she had an operation to fuse the prolapsed discs, which was only partially successful. After my own diagnosis we were bound by a shared experience of other people's

indifference to pain they had not, themselves, felt. Debbie's condition seemed to be specifically designed to force her to drop the smiling mask and speak up. She became an expert at navigating the country of illness, and often helped me find my way. She stopped dancing in 1989 when she was injured in rehearsals for *How on Earth*. Years later I was startled to be reminded by her that I had been the one that caught her in an awkward position; I didn't drop her but she slipped slightly from my grasp and the base of her spine landed hard on my thigh. Although the degeneration of her spine had been a gradual erosion, I felt responsible.

Despite the success of my dancing and choreography, and my allies, in Limbs I was the paranoid fly in the ointment, determined not to be an honorary heterosexual, tediously insisting on my difference, and there were fights. All this is ancient history but although I was grateful for what Limbs taught me, when I left in 1983 to study in New York I was in search of something more substantial.

A year before I left, when Limbs was at the American Dance Festival in North Carolina, I had a peculiar experience. One night I dreamt I was standing behind someone rubbing the back of their head. This person's hair was short and ragged, with great chunks missing and bits sticking out. As the alarm went off for my early morning class, the dream speeded up like water going down a plughole, and as I woke, the person turned to face me. It was Malcolm's face that cross-faded into the hot Southern dawn, with the magnolia blossoms outside my window exhaling the dream's perfume. That night we talked on the phone and when I asked him how he was he said, 'I'm glad you can't see me because yesterday I cut my hair short and it's a fucking mess.'

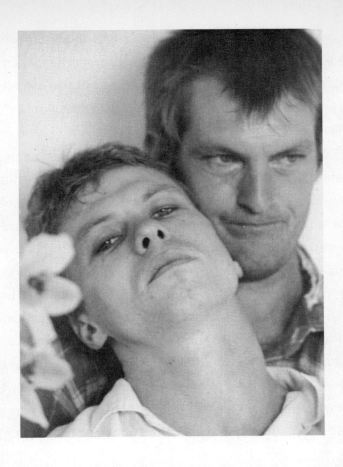

But my extra-sensory powers were limited; when I saw the Paul Taylor Company perform at the Festival I was deeply impressed, not dreaming for an instant that within a year I would be up there with them. That night their performance was filmed live for *Dance in America* and I distinctly remember one of the women falling over in Paul's cartoon version of the *Rite of Spring*. At the time she got up again so fast her fall barely registered, but later, after I'd joined the company, we used the video of that performance to learn our parts and we laughed ourselves sick as we played and replayed the moment when Linda hit the deck. Each time we rewound and played it again, it seemed inconceivable that the girl heading purposefully round the corner hadn't worked out by now how to prevent the fall, and with each repetition she looked so increasingly innocent, so determinedly dumb, just before she slipped, that we kept watching it until we were rolling on the floor in agonies of *Schadenfreude*.

But Linda falling over was not how I remembered that night. At the end of *Sacré*, everybody stabbed everybody else to death, one after another, in a mass 'et tu Brute?', until the only person left alive was the woman in white with her doll-baby balanced on her knee. The person who had just been killed was lying in front of them and in a tiny gap in the music her arm reached up with its dagger and then, perfectly in time with a single piano note, it stabbed the baby, once. Then the woman in white let her dead baby fall and began to dance the sacrificial solo to Stravinsky's primeval, stabbing score. She danced in a way I'd never seen, with the space around her body wrung into hieroglyphs of monumental grief, and although the audience tittered when the doll-baby was killed, as Ruth danced she made us forget our embarrassment and remember something else.

White Maori

After stumbling out of a thicket of past tenses I find myself wondering not where, but when I am. Even though I started late, I caught up and for quite a while was even a little ahead. Now I'm so late I'm *the* late.

When Malcolm and I left Whitaker Place the wax-man in the foyer was cut in half and taken with us. The bottom part was melted and the top was refashioned in my own image. Wax is a sensitive material; if you touch it, it lightens in colour, but if left alone it darkens to a honey-brown and over time keeps darkening, unless you touch it again. Malcolm keeps this moody Narcissus out of sight, like a broken barometer. He still has it, and every now and then when I'm visiting I walk into a spare room and surprise myself.

At some point, after I joined Limbs, we opened up our relationship so we could see others, if we wanted. The initial fire had settled to a kind of pilot-flame, but there were violent flashes of jealousy on both sides when we strayed. My years in New York put an end to our physical intimacy, but after I returned, it was obvious that our bond was, mutually, essential.

In 1990 I stopped drinking and although Malcolm and I went our separate ways we were as close as ever. In fact he assumed responsibility for my drinking duties and drank twice as much. While I focused on my work he kept losing jobs and ended up on a benefit. Unable to keep up the mortgage repayments on his house in Arch Hill he sold it for a song and began renting the cheapest flats he could find. He was still constantly writing and creating, but could never quite bring himself to finish anything and became a master of self-sabotage and procrastination. After I moved back to Auckland in 1991 we lived close to each other and whenever I visited it seemed he was getting thinner and more uncared for, so that at one point he looked like the one with Aids. For a few weeks he had nowhere to go and stayed with me. It was a disaster and it was then I discovered Malcolm was waging a secret war against me. My patu disappeared and later turned up at his place with all its carving whittled off. Someone I'd never seen knocked on the door in the middle of the night and began to abuse and threaten me for the shabby way I treated Malcolm. Once or twice Malcolm said things to me that were so hateful it took my breath away. When I asked him why, what, when, he clammed up or, if he was intoxicated enough, gave me a glimpse of a seething list of wrongs I had perpetrated on him. It felt like he had a little doll of me, moulded from all my wrongs, and toyed with it, sticking pins in it, while he stewed over what had been done to him. I wasn't the only one who had let him down badly, just the handiest.

He was, as ever, preoccupied with the past, particularly his family, and his father was the big scratch in his stuck record. After his mother died the bulk of his inheritance was entrusted to his still-living father who kept Malcolm in a state of penury while he himself developed a senile obsession with the latest gadgets. He had 20 wrist-watches, 20 toasters, 20 electric jugs, 5 microwave ovens, 3 lawn-mowers and 8 vacuum cleaners while Malcolm sometimes didn't have enough to eat, though he always seemed to have more than enough to drink. Malcolm's teeth were rotting and he divested himself of all his possessions except for a photograph of his mother; another nineteenth-century photograph of two old Maori men with a Pakeha gentleman; one of me; the wax bust; and hundreds of paperback cookbooks lined up beside his single mattress on the bare floorboards as if reading recipes could nourish the thing inside him that was starving. Mirrors were banished. The legend of his beauty

was bound and gagged. He still painted but without enthusiasm; mostly he painted pornography for a select clientele who weren't interested in his other work. He was possessed with a pathological need to blame his father for everything. I tried to help him but not hard enough and I had to tell him if he mentioned his father or brother again I would scream. The house he was living in was infested with fleas and Malcolm was like a man frozen in a dream, immobilised by a sclerosis of grudges.

Poor Istina seemed to be suffering from the same affliction. At that time she was a flea-ridden scrap of whining tortoiseshell always biting herself, and although I killed all her fleas they kept coming back until finally she disappeared, crawling under the house to die, at the cat age of 105.

While browsing I came across this passage in the previously quoted *Maori Wars of The Nineteenth Century* by S. Percy Smith that seems, if I substitute 'Malcolm' for 'Maori', oddly relevant to that time:

'Those of my readers who have had the patience to follow this history, so far, will have learnt that revenge has been the guiding principle which led to the events that have been related. If [Malcolm] can be said to have any sense of duty at all, it is – or perhaps were better put, was – the enduring feeling that any injury inflicted on his family or tribe must be satisfied by utu, exacted to the uttermost limit. It was a feeling that might slumber even for generations, but in the end its rigorous fulfilment was the corner-stone of [Malcolm's] honour. In relating in brief form the histories, the learned man will give a strict debtor and creditor account starting with the origin and follow it up by naming those who sacrificed on either side, alternately, in settlement of the account.'

Eventually in the dead of night Malcolm fell, broke his ribs and punctured his lung and after getting out of hospital was drawn back up north where his father and brother still lived, as if by a powerful magnet. About a year later his father died, the spell was partially broken, and Malcolm had enough money to buy a state house in a predominantly Maori suburb of Whangarei, where he still lives. Although he keeps his father in a kind of concentration camp of memory, all the signs are that his mother is being rehabilitated and punctiliously forgiven. The photograph of her as a young, beautiful woman, someone not yet tainted by association with his father, has beamed down its promise of fulfilment from Malcolm's walls for decades. Her 1971 analysis of the Treaty of Waitangi, our founding document, took years to find acceptance. She focused on the differences in meaning between the English and the Maori versions, noting that certain crucial words did not tally. Apparently one Maori chief at first supposed that 'the shadow of the land' would go to Queen Victoria 'but the substance will remain with us'. He soon realised it was to be the other way around.

These days Malcolm is busy trying to solve a mystery his mother set him on her death-bed, as her dying wish.

Ruth Ross died of cancer in 1982. It's a measure of my self-absorption and guilt at abandoning Malcolm that I remember her as dying after I went to New York, in 1983, not before I left. I do recall her and Malcolm's father coming to visit in mid-1982 when we were living in Scanlan Street, Ponsonby. She was ill then, but still imposing. Malcolm looks a lot like his mother, who looks a lot like mine, though my mother has black hair and Ruth was not quite blonde; blue-eyed, with classic Aryan good looks and prominent bones, even before her illness. I remember Malcolm taking me to their house in Weymouth for a visit. My first sight of Ruth was of her coming in from the garden with a spade in her hand and an abstracted, swaggering air, as if she had been interrupted in the unearthing of an important archaeological find, perhaps the bones of a moa. That first impression was momentary; she was entirely present, cordial, though still a little remote. In conversation, she had the disconcerting habit of rolling her eyeballs back in her head, so, briefly, all you could see were the flickering whites as she scanned her brain-dictionary. *Autochthonous* was the academic word for *tangata whenua*. I knew she was a historian and, later, when I was helping her with the dishes I tried to think of something historical to say, asking if she had seen the TV series *I, Claudius*. I didn't realise the importance of the visit to Malcolm. He said afterwards in wonderment, 'My mother kissed you.' His father was shorter, but puffed up, a kind of rooster who managed to give the impression he was present while keeping us at a safe distance with short, gruff remarks. I ran into him in town one day after that and when he realised there was no escape he asked in a strangulated voice, 'How's the bach?' For an instant I couldn't think what he was talking about and then it dawned on me he was referring to the impossible place where Malcolm and I lived together.

Some time that year, when I was away on tour with Limbs, a new flatmate called Dawn moved into the big old villa in Scanlan Street. She was acting in *Get the hell home, boy*, a play by Selwyn Muru and, on the last night, invited the cast back for a party. As Malcolm tells it, he had been visiting his sick mother in Weymouth and arrived back late to find the party in full swing. The door was opened by Te Paki Cherrington who said, 'Who are you?' to which Malcolm replied, 'I live here.' He was then treated like manuhiri, an honoured guest, and ceremonially ushered in. During the evening Selwyn Muru talked about his next play, the story of an ordained Maori clergyman who reverted to the old gods. The following weekend when Malcolm was visiting his mother again he started telling her

216

about it. She kept interrupting and talking at cross purposes and Malcolm was starting to lose his patience when he realised she was talking in parallel. Ruth was trying to tell him about Pirimona Te Kariri (Philomon the Scribe), a Maori clergyman whose name she had come across in a variety of contexts over twenty years researching missionary history, piecing together the outline of a strange and disturbing story. Pirimona's origins were deeply obscure, she told him. The date and place of his birth, even his tribal affiliations, are unknown. He was educated at the Waimate mission school and from there went on to St John's College to study theology. He was a distinguished student and was ordained in 1861. In 1863 when Pirimona was a minister in a Christchurch parish, General Cameron, acting on orders from Governor Grey, crossed the Mangatawhiri in a declaration of war. This invasion of the Waikato was effectively a land grab; any resistance by local Maori was taken as a pretext for confiscation.

Ruth was dying and Malcolm was aware that if she stayed up late she'd suffer for it the next day and he kept urging her to go to bed. 'Oh shut up,' she said, 'I'm enjoying myself.' As news of the invasion spread Pirimona became a vocal critic of the government's war policy. He left his parish and wife and child and 'went bush' on a speaking tour from marae to marae, contesting the war, heading north in a journey away from the Anglican Church and towards the gods of his ancestors. It seems he couldn't reconcile within himself the great gap between the newspaper reports of what had happened and the accounts he was hearing from his own people. The Church had lost him and while he was out of sight there was a call in the House of Representatives for him to be tried for sedition. The problem for Governor Grey was that if Pirimona was arrested and tried it would have been a huge political embarrassment because it would be putting the war itself on trial, a war that couldn't stand too close a scrutiny. There is even the possibility Pirimona himself was aware of that and was angling to be put on trial himself. He emerged from the bush in Mangonui where he agreed to give a statement to the local magistrate to explain his actions. Pirimona kept the appointment but refused to make his statement in English, giving it instead in Maori. As an ordained minister he was perfectly conversant with English and possibly also had Latin and Greek, since he had been academically brilliant. As Malcolm told me, the statement itself was, in his mother's words, 'a cry from the heart'. The fact that he 'declined to speak the tongue' showed he had lost faith in English institutions. That was in November 1863. The statement was translated and conveyed to the government and subsequently published. His wife was awarded a widow's pension by the Anglican Church in April 1864. The next reference comes 40 years later in Lady Martin's reminiscences, where she says he was drowned. Up until his death Pirimona aroused a hysterical reaction and then there was complete silence. His life and death were equally embarrassing: his death was too convenient; in that climate assassination would be easy to facilitate and impossible to prove. Where was he drowned? Nobody knew. Ruth thought Selwyn Muru's play was a folk-memory of the story of Pirimona Te Kariri.

When she had finished telling Malcolm the story she said, 'Well, what are you going to do with it?' and although he wanted to give her some reassurance he could only reply, 'I don't know.' He felt his mother was identifying with Pirimona's crisis of faith, as she, a committed atheist, prepared herself to 'meet her maker' or not. Her own discovery of the discrepancies between the English and Maori versions of the Treaty were a further point of identification. The 'shadow of the land' was part of Malcolm's inheritance. This was effectively their last conversation since after that his mother was paralysed and couldn't speak although, as he told me, towards the end she tried to count aloud but could only ever get up to nine. Then she would ask, 'What comes after nine?' and was oblivious of ten.

He was telling me what his mother had told him in 1982, over twenty years later in the kitchen of his house in Otangerei. I had driven up to see him and continue our talk. The day before we had visited the site of the battle of Te Ika-a-ranganui, which is marked by a small obelisk. There was nothing there, apart from trees, grass and wind. A shining cuckoo sharpened the silence. Further east we stopped again, to get a better view of the lay of the land and Malcolm unfolded a map and pointed out the direction of Poutu and where the war parties had come from. Now, sitting in his kitchen, I was taking notes with a pink ballpoint pen with the words *Huddleston Hypnotherapy – Positively Helping* on it. There was a greasy yellow fly-swatter on the windowsill beside me, complete with squashed fly. Next to it was a fly on its back feebly kicking its legs in the air, dying from an overdose of flyspray. Actually the room was rancid with flies.

Malcolm is the only Pakeha in the street and it occurred to me that his neighbours were the same people he had grown up with, now graduated from rural poverty to suburban despair. The kitchen window looked out on the road. It was like a stage set with old Maori ladies ambling past with their wide-eyed mokopuna, prepubescent gangsta rappers hiphopping along and cars driving up in clouds of Bob Marley and dope, then screeching off again. I felt ridiculously exposed, my head and shoulders like the profile of the Queen on a coin. Nobody seemed to be taking the slightest notice of me but I knew they were all well known to Malcolm. On his workroom wall there was a row of beautiful flax kete, hand-woven by one of his neighbours and every now and then someone knocked at the door and Malcolm would give them twenty dollars for the cleaning, or the lawns, or until next week and then he nipped out to the ATM to get some money for Mel and I bit my tongue.

He brought out a folder of his files on Pirimona and other related research. Malcolm has not yet solved the mystery of the Scribe's death but thinks he is getting closer. He says it's hard to know how wide to cast the net because information is so scattered it can come from the unlikeliest quarters. One of the things he discovered was a letter from a Ms Weale to Bishop Selwyn concerning the Maori party that visited London in 1863. In it she mentions that one of the party, Reihana Te Taukawau, 'was never weary of talking about' his great friend the 'Native Clergyman – Pirimona'. Unfortunately the letter says no more on that subject. Doratea Charlotte Julia Weale was a maiden lady from Dorset, an heiress and lay missionary involved with the 'Aboriginie Protection Society', an all-round campaigner for the rights of those less fortunate than herself. Malcolm gave me her long letter to read. It was passionately articulate, a torrent of strictly controlled outrage on behalf of the Maori who had been brought to London to be exhibited under false pretences. In New Zealand the Maori of the time were raised under a programmatic suppression of their 'heathen customs' and it was a bizarre and interesting fact that the upholsterer and lay preacher William Jenkins had taught the 14 chosen Maori their own outlawed haka and waiata from a text compiled by another white man, a Mr C. O. Davis, so they could be taken to England and exhibited for money. It must have been an astonishing and comical sight to see this Pakeha correcting the Maori in their own traditional songs and dances on ship-deck. According to Malcolm, Jenkins went first-class and the performers went steerage, eating weevil-ridden biscuits. One of the party was Hariata Haumu. She was a last-minute add-on, wandering around Auckland in a deranged state, demanding to be taken. She went mad at sea and on arrival in London was committed. The spectacle of Victorian London must have been as terrifying to her as any hallucination. She died in England and was possibly the first Maori woman to be buried there, in a pauper's grave. She was a pathetic victim of what is now called post-colonial stress disorder, a pioneering Maori schizo-phrenic, or so Malcolm said.

MR. W. JENKINS, INTERPRETER. HOROMANA TE ATUA. HAPIMANA NGAPIKO. WHAREPAPA. POMARE. PARATENE TE MANU.
KIHIRINI TE TUAHU. TAKEREI NGAWAKA. TERE TE IRINGA. HARIATA POMARE. REIHANA TAUKAWAU. KIHINI PAKIA. NGAHUIA. WIREMU POU.
NATIVE CHIEFS FROM NEW ZEALAND.—SEE PAGE 74.

It was evident from Doratea's letter that she had a lot of affection for the Maori she was hosting and trying to help get back to New Zealand. Malcolm's face shone as he told me of her special regard for the old man Paratene te Manu who, when he was shown around the

Royal Zoo, offered to take on Queen Victoria's lions with his taiaha until it was explained that the Queen wouldn't be pleased if he killed them. I think Malcolm has been slightly sidetracked from his search for the answer to the mystery of the death of Pirimona Te Kariri by his discovery of Doratea Charlotte Julia Weale. Her letter reveals her formidable intellect, her steely will and her discerning heart. Malcolm is trying to find out more about her life, and is planning to write a book, but little is known of Doratea, although she tantalisingly reveals in one sentence that she did visit New Zealand some time before 1863. In some ways she is a Victorian version of his mother. They both revelled in a worthy austerity. Although Ruth was a twice-married atheist and Doratea was devout and almost certainly a virgin, I think Doratea was the more maternal. Malcolm has two xeroxed photographs of her. In the first, a *carte de visite*, she is 33, sitting on a carved chair wearing a bonnet tied under her chin in a large bow, shawled, gloved, clasping a little bag or reticule, with voluminous skirts that completely conceal her nether parts. She is looking slightly off to one side, her face beaky, determined, like an anxious mother duck or hen. In the later image, a *carte de cabinet*, she is 52 and is pictured with three Maori men; her look softened, the quacking bonnet settled into a white cap, she holds the little bag in the other hand. Although the men in the photograph are obviously of another race, with an elderly seated man the image's dignified centre, they look like the reunited members of a family at peace.

Not so with us. Malcolm and I argued about syntax and the relative merits of the first person versus the third. He was scathing of something I'd written and it felt as if he was standing to one side and giving me the full wintry blast of his parents' scorn of his own childhood efforts; a blast which blew me out of the room, into the car and all the way back to Auckland. I was so stunned I omitted the last wave in answer to the waving shadow in the kitchen, but did catch a glimpse of the wax sculpture of me as I was blown out. I remembered it as a bust but now there is only the head and neck, the colour of thunder, sitting on a toddler's chair in his bedroom.

When I got home Leo kept bringing me presents to cheer me up. I got two dead mice and half a screaming lizard.

– 18 –

Three pilgrimages and a burglar

In 1989 when I was in London filming *Dead Dreams* with DV8, the Paul Taylor Company came to Sadler's Wells Theatre for a season. I felt like a movie star when I drove up in a taxi on opening night to see a blown-up photograph of me dancing in *Arden Court* on one of the banners outside. My friend Michelle who was with me caught me flicking back my hair just as I was getting out of the taxi and we both snorted in disgust at my vanity. Paul was standing in the foyer in a tuxedo waiting for Lady-somebody-or-other who was to grace us with her presence that night. He radiated fury and stood completely still, like a wax replica of himself, or someone in an avant-garde performance. A complicated smile hovered like a wasp over his mouth and he completely failed to see me or return my greeting. It was strange watching the family I'd left performing the same old rituals. The work seemed tarnished although Kate still danced like real royalty and one of the new works was so corny I cringed in my seat and Lloyd's eyes lit up. As I left I mumbled a few complimentary words to Paul and Bettie and they mumbled back. It was a crisis.

After the season Chris and Ginger, the costume lady, were hiring a car and touring Wales and Cornwall and they asked me to join them. Ginger is small and pale ginger, with a round plain face, glasses, a sympathetic nature and a razor wit. She was easy to overlook in the company of dancers, a sparrow among the swans and parakeets, but there is a gold thread running through her. She likes to sing hymns. As far as I could tell, Ginger was now in love with the devoutly homosexual Chris. He accepted this homage; they seemed to have a tacit agreement and had become 'best friends'. It was an unlikely alliance, and yet oddly fitting, with a gold thread running

through it. Ginger favours buttons and bows and frills, and always reminds me of Jane Austen with an American accent. Chris, on the other hand, was an All-American Canadian, Clark Kent by day and Superman on stage at night. Apart from a one-night stand our relationship was musical. For four years we danced the exhausting duet in *Arden Court*. It is a rollicking, jousting dance with a lot of unison and the different way we interpreted the music intensified the aura of fraternal rivalry. Chris liked to be on the leading edge of the dot of the note and I liked to be bang in the middle or even on the opposite rim of its circumference. At one point we exited the stage at exactly the same time as the music finished, then waited for a breath in the wings before re-entering, the choreography requiring that we hit the first note of the next section of music in mid-flight. When dancing to recorded music we knew exactly how long the interval of silence was, but when we had an orchestra we often came out too early and had to wait in the air for the conductor to join us. We became so attuned to each other we could even make mistakes in near-perfect unison.

Chris had a comic-strip take on the world and my major memory of that trip is of he and I standing in front of sacred stone circles, or the Iron Age hillside chalk-drawing of a giant with an erection, with Ginger taking our picture, and at the last moment while I looked serious and spiritual, Chris stuck his finger out of his undone fly or pretended he was holding up the huge dolmen in the stone circle. The Cerne Giant is a colossus, outlined in white chalk against the green grass of Giant Hill and the guidebook told us he stands 55 metres high, with a 37-metre club in his right hand and displays both testicles and an erect phallus seven metres long. In the eighteenth century it was believed the Giant lived upon human flesh and had rashers of baby for breakfast and in the evening slipped down the hillside for a drink at the river and to catch and eat virgins.

Apparently whole books have been written about the history of prudery with the appearance and the disappearance and then the reappearance of the Giant's genitals over the centuries as the measuring rod. White witches were known to worship him as a fertility god but his origins are a mystery. We went to the ruins of Glastonbury Cathedral and to Bath, drinking from sacred healing springs dedicated to Minerva, and one night, stoned on hash, we wandered over the monstrous, moonlit boulders at Lyme Regis as the sea crashed around us. There were inscrutable faces slumbering in the moon-shadowed stones, with tresses of seaweed writhing about their briny skulls. We stayed there for hours that night, on the breakwater.

It was all romantic and pagan and Ginger's eyes grazed on Chris as he pranked and spoofed along the ley-lines. Chris explained that ley-lines were straight lines of spiritual energy marked out by sequences of ancient monuments from the time of the Druids, and we were following them. We stayed in damp bed and breakfasts in Welsh towns with names too long to say in one breath and drank beer in the rain with violet-coloured cows watching us. It wasn't until the end of the trip that Ginger confided in me that Chris had Aids and this was his pilgrimage.

In 1998 I found myself in the same part of England, in Somerset, being driven by a long-haired male disciple to the Mother Centre of the meditation I now practise. He mentioned in passing that according to legend, King Arthur and the Knights of the Round Table had lived in the area, and it reminded me of Chris. I had persevered with the Buddhist meditation two hours daily for several years but had found it too dry and arduous; there were no more eruptions. By coincidence Ann, a dancer friend, was involved with a meditation and healing Centre at Leigh north of Auckland where I learnt a different form of yoga. It is based on a secret mantra and other

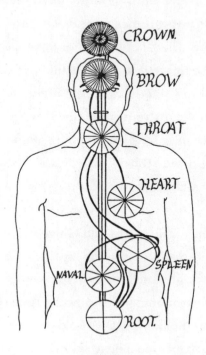

visualisations and it gave me little sips of something that both quenched and reawakened my thirst for bliss. The only difficulty was that in every room there was a picture of a middle-aged Englishwoman, her hands clasped in prayer, and some of the people at the Centre bowed to this picture before and after meditation. There were other photographs of Indian men who were also bowed to. I ignored this for a while until I had to face the fact that this woman with a turned-up nose and a holy expression was Mataji Yogananda, the guru and founder of the Centre. The ancient Indian meditation she passed on to us through our teachers was given to her by beings that existed on another plane. Oh dear. When Malcolm caught sight of her photograph on the cover of a magazine I had, without knowing who she was he dubbed her 'that stuck-up bitch'. But I loved the meditation and after three years practising it I decided to go to the Mother Centre for a course and hopefully to meet Mataji.

The Centre is in a small thatch-roofed village in Yeoville called Queen Camel. It consists of several buildings all grouped around an old Tudor farmhouse; Owl Cottage for Mataji and her husband, the main house for 'the family', one for healing, two for meditation, and the guest building. There was a garden full of peony roses, a pond fat with goldfish, a dovecote with several large white doves in angelic residence, and a hush in the air. The car tyres crunched on the gravel as we arrived and I held my breath. I was shown to my room and that night at dinner met the others who had come for the five-day course. We were served by an older woman whose face was like a micro-scopically observed etching by Dürer of the battle between anger and the desire to please. As we ate, a shadow passed over me and I was suddenly suffocated with fear. I put my head down and pretended to eat, trying to tough it out as the others chatted happily but then I identified a needle sharp pain under my arm as the beginning of shingles. Since that first agonising bout in 1987 I had been taking medication to keep it at bay, but when I was exhausted it sometimes threatened to break through the drug prophylactic and then I needed to triple the dose and rest. I excused myself, found the man who had driven me and told him I was ill and wouldn't be able to do the course.

So I stayed in my room and meals were sent up, one with a little note from Mataji saying for me to go to the small meditation room in the afternoon and I would receive a blessing. I didn't know what a blessing was but went and sat in the exquisite little octagonal room with stained-glass windows and the usual pictures. It was like sitting inside a priceless oriental vase and I began to meditate as I had been taught. After a few minutes I felt an extremely odd sensation. It was as if a fat tongue of light was being pushed through the top of my head. It slithered down and fiddled with my heart and then dived right to the base of my spine, kindled and lit a fire there that exploded into an ecstatic bonfire. I sat there for I don't know how long with the flames like a lion roaring inside me. All I remember is stumbling around outside in the garden afterwards amazed at how alive and funny everything was. There was a big golden fish swimming in the pond and I could feel it wriggling like a re-attached amputated limb I'd got so used to being separated from that I mistook the pain of its absence for reality. Now I could move it again. For the next few weeks I felt as though my breastbone was soaked in honey and hummingbirds were drinking from it, their beating wings fanning the flames of this weird ecstasy. I went for long walks around Queen Camel, often seeing people approaching from quite a distance and despite my newfound bliss I still worried whether or not I should greet them. I had an appointment to meet Mataji and when she came in she was the lady in the picture. She hugged me, saying, 'Let me look at you,' and then held me at arm's length. It was like being looked at by the full moon and the last wisps of my cynicism disappeared. Then she said, 'Oh, I think you should just say hello to them and if they don't answer, never mind. That's their problem.' We both laughed and outside it rained and rained and Mataji closed the windows as she murmured a compliment to the sky. We talked for a while and then she left, walking slowly as her long paisley gown fluttered in the wind. I could see her ivory-white shins as she crunched on the gravel.

The state of being made love to by something I thought must be God followed me all the way back to London, to Brussels and Prague where I spent most of my time meditating in my dinky hotel room, shuddering so hard with joy I thought I'd get whiplash. I was trying with all my might to surrender, to feed myself to the light, but kept finding that the part of me that was trying so hard was also the very thing holding me back. In Brussels there was a fountain I couldn't pass without swooning; its flowering gush so perfectly mirrored what was oh-so-nearly happening inside me. In Prague I saw a painting by El Greco, a head of Jesus that seemed to be breathing. And on my last stop in Thailand I visited the Buddhist temples where I could feel and see the Bliss as if it was a swarm of diamond-flies clustered around piles of holy shit. Once back in Auckland as the ecstasy faded I quickly set to work on *Arc*, the dance it had seeded, and grew my hair long, in my idea of a mystic. It's odd but today, just before I wrote this, I got a letter from 'that stuck-up bitch' Mataji and a phone call from Janet.

The meditation Centre at Leigh closed recently. For several years I spent each Christmas and often Easter breaks on retreat there, 'in the silence'. I love not speaking. The Centre was run by Laugharnananda, an Englishwoman who lived there. She had long white hair, floated about in pristine white, amethyst and fringed turquoise, and was brimful of a sometimes irritating humility and good cheer. Laugharnananda was my meditation teacher and had a meticulous sense of humour. She was the conduit of a benevolence that was mother's-milk and I found sanctuary at the Centre in Leigh. Now it is closed and Laugharnananda has gone back to England, I miss both her and it. Mataji said in her letter that centres are 'only bricks and mortar', and that meditation is the true home. I'm thankful to have been given the technique. It keeps me from going under.

I remember after my first retreat, driving back to Auckland, having to keep blinking hard to convince myself the real world was real. Driving refocused my old whining brain and as I approached home, out of habit, I began to worry. As I drove up the driveway, my next-door neighbour rushed out of her house as if she'd been waiting for me. She was a pleasant woman with a large family of boys and though we were civil, I was always aware of her noticing that I involuntarily licked my chops whenever I saw her eldest. So she was wary. But now she ran up to the car as I parked.

'Oh,' she said, 'I thought I heard glass breaking a little while ago and I should have done something. I'm so sorry. I don't know, maybe someone ...'

We rushed to my front door and as I stuck the key in the lock I heard the sound of rats with soft-voiced sneakers running away. I think I fake-fumbled slightly to give them time. Mrs Malone was hot on my heels as I opened the door. I could see down the hallway that the back door was gaping and the place was a mess. All the cupboards and drawers were emptied onto the floor in heaps – piles of rag-and-bone rubbish I vaguely recognised as my life.

'Oh my God!' she said. She was right behind me as we turned into the lounge. I think I saw it just before she did but it took me a nanosecond to realise what I was looking at. In the first collision of images I got confused and thought it was the burglar on the television, and was about to turn-tail. Then I realised it was one of my porn videos, *Black and Hung*, I think, or possibly *The Bigger the Better*, playing on the screen with the sound turned off. As we entered the living-room a young black man with a huge erection turned lazily to face us; it was a mid-shot, thigh to head, in profile to give the full effect of his truly remarkable penis, almost a foot long like a strong baby's arm. I made a kamikaze dive for the power button and switched it off but I could tell from the little gasp behind me that Mrs Malone had just had all her fears confirmed in technicolour. She sort of backed away, clucking and making apologetic noises, leaving me to clean up the mess and call the police. Nothing had been stolen though it took me a while to regain my sense of holiness.

The last time I saw Tobias was in Ubud, Bali, in 2000. He was lecturing on a cruise ship that took millionaires to exotic places. Tobias was their resident Asmat expert, thrilling all the blue-rinsed old ladies and their laconic husbands with his head-hunting, cock-sucking *schtick*. He was mildly ashamed at this exploitation of the tribe he loved but reasoned that at least he knew how to stop the tourists from doing their worst. We arranged to meet in a fancy hotel he knew and I arrived a day or two before him. I found Bali sinister, as if the blinding smiles were hiding something dark coiled underneath. There was a lot of smiling in Bali. In the monkey forest the tourists smiled bravely and took each other's photographs as the sidling anthropoids picked their pockets for food and pulled their hair. At night when I had to walk through this forest to get back to the hotel, the monkeys shadowed me in the trees overhead and occasionally one scampered across my path as I fought the impulse to run. I remember lying in my $200-a-night suite, complete with Balinese antiques and feeling depressed. I looked out the window at some people working in the hot sun in the rice paddies and realised they were labouring so I could be depressed in luxury. It seemed the more you paid, the more immaculately dressed and gorgeous Balinese clustered around you, smiling loudly, to make sure you were having fun. They seemed to have no idea of the pleasures of solitude and constantly asked me where I was going that day, looking shocked and upset at my 'nowhere'. Didn't I want to see their beautiful country? I was wandering around the luscious tropical gardens one afternoon, trying to look as if I was having fun, when I came across an old man with a cane. We looked at each other in wonder until we realised he was Tobias and I was Douglas. We fell into each other's arms and laughed at how much we'd changed, although the bond between us was the same.

Over the next week we hired air-conditioned cars and drove to exotic gardens and zoos with recreated rainforests that had been ripped out, complete with the startled creatures, from their native habitat for our pleasure. At one point I found myself standing with Tobias, by virtue of a slowly ascending spiral ramp, high up in the canopy of the Asmat jungle with birds of paradise whizzing past our heads and other native flora and fauna that Tobias murmured the native names of under his breath, as if he was dreaming. We visited a museum with an unintentionally frightening exhibition of paintings done by Balinese of local scenes in the gory styles of Van Gogh and Picasso. At the hotel Tobias was treated like a king; they had known him for years. His toad-hands shook and his wisp of hair was ashen but he still called me 'darling' with the tremor of love in his voice. He was 80, had Parkinson's and his memory was going. With his two (or is it three?) hip operations he found it hard to get around, let alone to remember the name or place that was on the tip of his tongue. 'Dammit!' he'd say as he forgot again.

The streets in Ubud were hell; pedestrians had to run between the constant traffic, choking on the fumes, and Tobias couldn't run. I remember standing on the side of the road with him waiting for a gap big enough for him to hobble across with my help but the gap never came. So I finally strode out into the middle of the road, put both hands out and screamed at the cars to stop which they did in amazement at my sacrilege. I felt like Moses parting the Red Sea as Tobias limped across the road, a radiant smile on his face. We had a lovely lunch, no chilli for me and lots for Tobias. He likes it hot. He told me how this was his last cruise because he couldn't remember

his lectures any more and described how he'd been singing his favourite Asmat song about the little shrimp to the tourists, the song the men sing which goes:

> Sisi ya,
> yuwa sisi ya,
> asa korama, yi korama,
> nana sisi wow, nana sisi wow,
> yi! yi!

and means:

There are shrimp in the small river,
there are shrimp,
they clean the shit, they clean the piss,
we eat the shrimp, we eat the shrimp,
yi! yi!

and when he came to the translation he forgot what the song meant and got all mixed up and confused and had to start all over again, only to forget again. Tobias had sung the song for me before and loved to act out the paddling movements of the men in the canoe as he sang, as if he was back in the jungle living his dream of an untamed world of wild men. But the passengers on the cruise had been 'darling' and everybody gave him a standing ovation but only because this was the end. Even before we parted I felt in my heart that Tobias was already on his way to join the remotest tribe in human history.

– 19 –

Seahorsing

In the published diaries of the late Kurt Cobain there's a drawing he did of a design for a tee-shirt with a seahorse on it. Written beside the drawing are words to the effect that amongst all living creatures, seahorses are the only species in which the male becomes pregnant, carries the eggs to maturity and gives birth. I've always been fascinated with the idea of men giving birth, tracing my interest back to an episode of the TV programme *Bewitched* I saw when I was a kid. In this episode Darren dreams he is the first man on the planet to have a baby and we see him lying in a hospital bed surrounded by reporters and television cameras, cradling the newborn (human) infant with his proud witch-wife, Samantha, at the bedside.

Looking further into the enigma of the seahorse I discovered they are masters of camouflage, able to change colour to match their surroundings in a matter of minutes. One book notes that 'one individual even turned fluorescent orange to blend with a piece of flagging tape used to mark out a scientific plot'. They are also able to grow, at will, fleshy appendages to imitate seaweed or the fronds of algae that they cling to in the hope of outwitting their most vigilant predator, the human being. Pliny, in his *Natural History* says, 'Hair lost through mange is restored by ashes of the sea-horse, either mixed with soda and pig's lard, or else by itself in vinegar ... Sea-horses are killed in rose-oil, to make ointment for those sick of chill fevers, and sea-horses themselves are worn as an amulet by the patient.' They were also thought to cure rabies. But the vast majority are used in traditional Chinese medicine, often to treat sexual disorders and as aphrodisiacs. I have a dried seahorse I bought in Venice; it looks like an elegant shrivelled foetus.

When I read, standing in the bookshop, the entry in Kurt Cobain's diary I was thrilled at the confirmation that males can and do give birth, and in the same way as when I see a herd of cows on my walks through Cornwall Park I want to lie down in the paddock and join them, now in the evenings when I'm clinging with my tail to the frond of the couch, I like to imagine I'm a seahorse resting after giving birth. Although most of my offspring are now deceased, some are only sleeping, yet others were stillborn, but they were all given equal attention. I think this talent for self-dramatisation I get from my father who was an extremely butch drama-queen. He once wrote me a letter complaining that the rum on the island where he was living was forcing him to drink it. I know what he means. Finding those letters from him, from 'your poor old Dad', was like hearing an old song that, without noticing it, I had been singing for years, although in a different key and hopefully, with more variations.

Once settled back in New Zealand I formed a company and began to labour. Jim died, Chris died, my older brother Phillip was killed on his motorbike, my cousin Christopher took his own life, and other friends died while they were still new. Whenever the phone rang in the middle of the night I cringed. At first all my friends seemed to be dying elsewhere and I couldn't quite believe they were gone. I had to make dances to convince myself. Then Warren, an old lover, had a severe allergic reaction to one of the Aids drugs and I went down to Wellington to see him.

When I first came into the hospital room I touched the lump on the bed where his foot was and he screamed with pain. His entire body was experiencing some monstrous mutation of the localised bout of shingles I had had. Even Warren's eyelids were cauterised. Over the following weeks he lay under a thin veil of morphine and suffered a mortification I found impossible to comprehend even though it was taking place right in front of me. It was as if, while never leaving his bed, he was travelling barefoot through bloated, festering rainforests, crossing sizzling deserts, climbing mountains of thorns, shivering in polar blizzards, walking on razor-sharp coral at the bottom of the sea, being kept alive so yet another plague could be manifest. After a while he seemed to stop travelling and his body itself became the inhuman landscape he had arrived at. Apparently there was nothing anyone could do except administer as much morphine as possible without killing him. To sit with him was to experience claustrophobia and agoraphobia at the same time; he was both suffocatingly close and as far away as a stone orbiting the carnivorous sun of another galaxy. At one point I was sitting staring at his immobile face when the sound of the fan turned into a movie-projector and I saw projected onto Warren's face in quick succession a series of masks; Medieval Christs, a *femme fatale*, a punk rocker, an emaciated monk with a face suffused with kindness, a monkey, a demon, his mother, and then underneath them all, a skull, trembling to the surface. Then his face really was moving and he made funny little grunts and moans, drawing his lips back in a sneer, a smile, his breathing rapid and shallow. His eyes fluttered, then, like butterfly wings glued together, stickily opened and he struggled to the surface and saw me.

'It's Douglas,' I said.

'Douglas,' he said politely. 'How are you?'

'I'm good,' and then stupidly, 'how are you?'

'Bad breath,' he exhaled it. 'Could you do something for me?'

'Yes,' I said eagerly. Then he whispered something I had to get him to repeat. It was a Latin word and I had no idea of its meaning but ran carrying it, like a lit match, to Linda, the nurse who was in the other room. And it turned out the word was the name of the medicine to help clear the cobweb of white thrush that was clogging

240

his throat and Linda came in and fed him it with a little eyedropper as if he was a baby bird.

When he finally died and we unwrapped and washed him, we found something that bore no resemblance to our mischievous friend; it was the shrunken remains of an ancient, wizened alien annihilated by exposure to the environment we called friendly. Outside the window, as we cleaned him, I could see the sunny beaches of Wellington, the blue sky and the blue sea, but I couldn't believe in them. That summer the pohutukawas in blossom were intensely vivid, and walking back to Linda's the hills looked to me as if they were haemorrhaging.

Not long after his death I dreamt I saw Warren in the arrival hall of an airport, at the point of immigration. There was a long line of people waiting to be processed and Warren was officiating, standing at the booth, his hair dyed blond, laughing and giving everyone cheek as he stamped their passports and waved them through.

During the drawn-out process of his dying one or two of his friends made themselves scarce. This was in 1994 when Aids was still fashionable but it seemed that, for some, Warren's gruesome death was a serious breach of etiquette. Maybe they were just scared. When he kept asking after one person who had been close we made up stories and tried to persuade this person to visit. He finally came, clutching a Bible, as if entering a den of vampires.

After my own diagnosis I reproduced like a man with an urgent deadline. The works of dance theatre I made with the help of my collaborators between 1988 and 2002 read to me now like the names of the stages in a pilgrimage I didn't know I was making, or a list of songs nobody can remember the words to, belonging to a tribe that has disappeared. Dance is famously ephemeral; if unperformed the works survive as an echo, on video, in memory, or in name only.

– Now is the Hour –

– How on Earth –

– a far Cry –

– Passion Play –

– Gloria –

– As It Is –

– Elegy –

– Forever –

– The Decay of Lying –

– Buried Venus –

– Rose and fell –

– Forbidden Memories –

– Arc –

– halo –

– Anthem –

– Inland –

The birth of each work was painful, and afterwards it was as if I'd been hypnotised to forget how hard it had been and how I'd vowed never again. There were varying degrees of discomfort. Some works came out relatively easily, in hospitable environments with a lot of laughter, others were like crawling over broken glass through a war zone towards a bad review and a debt. But I had to follow my dream wherever it took me; it was a matter of survival and my dream was, for the most part, epic. It involved unusual combinations of dance, film, music, theatre and the spoken word. We drank water from each other's mouths, filmed a dinner party and its aftermath in the arms and massive root system of a Moreton Bay fig. People dropped from great heights, danced in counterpoint to their own projected images, sang ancient hymns, tore themselves to pieces like maenads, laughed at their own funerals, and wept real tears. When Kilda danced the solo in *How on Earth* she was like a moving caryatid, or one of those

trees so majestic, they're pillars that hold up the sky. And although Kilda responded to the gusts of music, bowing with the wind, there was at the same time a part of her that would never be moved. When she lowered her upraised arms, it was a command.

Technicians scrambled to find solutions to problems they'd never encountered, and I spent hours in darkened theatres being difficult, pulling my hair out as ill-prepared, underpaid, overworked crew fell over each other trying to make it work. It is a miracle that mostly it did. But it was much harder than I ever imagined possible and at times I had to make myself into a monster to get close to the desired result. It's a dubious pleasure to be feared by those around you.

Monsters are vulnerable. The last work crushed me and finally made me understand there would never be enough money in this country to buy the time needed to dream deep, even if I still had the energy. It was like having to give birth in five minutes, with the audience and critics waiting impatiently to snip the umbilical cord with their opinions, so they could move on to the next thing. One of the other dance-works at the Festival that year was from Brazil. They had been in rehearsal for over a year; we had six weeks. Humiliation is an effective deterrent.

Forever was a war we nearly won. When we performed it in Bern, Switzerland, the audience and critics gave us the kind of ovation that was like water falling on a desert. We were sold out and the people who couldn't get in watched outside on a video monitor. When they asked where we were going to next we had to tell them that more than 30 other festivals in Europe had rejected it. I had been naïve to believe I could remain a part of the international dance community from New Zealand. Festival producers looked down their noses and still couldn't see us. If they detected an unfashionable influence their noses twitched and it was instant banishment back to the colonies. Although we performed in Europe and Australia and were fleetingly acclaimed, we never broke into the international market, and by the time I realised I had failed to achieve my goal, that early ambition seemed to belong to 'a country far away as health'.

Here in New Zealand it was different. I was one of the lucky ones. The Arts Council, later renamed Creative New Zealand, supported my company as best they could. We had a small but enthusiastic audience that swelled and dwindled according to the winds of opinion. After I went public with my HIV status the theatres were crowded with the curious. For a time I felt like a freak in a gilded

cage, with the audience on the edge of its seat, waiting for me to die in time to the music. Eventually these disaster tourists lost interest and we were left with our loyal followers. And the critics. I was a genius, a disappointment, a dancing god, a spectacular failure, out to shock, morbid, boring, riveting, old-hat, hilarious, derivative and deeply moving. I had finally done it, or not, I couldn't tell. To get anybody to take their eyes off the rugby long enough to look at us sometimes seemed a miracle. When a cricket hero dropped a ball, thousands of people died in India.

At the end of 1999 there were articles in all the major New Zealand newspapers and magazines summing up achievements in the arts over the twentieth century. Not one I saw included dance as an art form. We exist in a blind spot.

And artists are such whingers.

The performers I worked with over the years were my precious raw material and each one brought to the work something incomparable: Kilda, Debbie, Brian, Shona, Alfred, Shona, Ann, Tai, Neil, Glenn, Mia, Sean, Sean, Marianne, Leonie, Darren, Daniel, Tane, Ursula, Lisa, David, Helaina, Helen, Claire, Matt, Raewyn, Jessica, Sarah, Sarah-Jayne, Ross, Craig, Kelly, Simon, Alexa, Ryan, Heto and the inimitable Peta Rutter. My longstanding designer Michael Pearce, of Melbourne, gave his all and worked magic with a pittance. Shona McCullagh, Ann Dewey, Fenn Gordon, rode shotgun, picked up the pieces, made me feel it was worth going on. Chloe, David Long, Chris Graves, John Verryt . . .

Every project bred its own microclimate of alliances, tiffs and flirtations and I was in the hot seat. Sometimes when a dancer left to do their own work we didn't speak for years. I think we're all speaking again now. For me dance has been cathartic; I went for the jugular, mining wounds for hidden treasure. Sometimes I came up with dross, at others we struck a vein. It was risky, and to perform at this pitch of intensity night after night is draining. Often I could

sense the audience as they got on our wavelength and rode the crest; on the rare occasions people laughed and cried at the same time, I was content. At other times I felt we were like those amputees hired to take part in filmed re-enactments of famous battles. Apparently they are given fake body parts and at a signal they press a button and their arms or legs explode as if they've just been blown off. According to my friend Chloe, who works in films, often these amputees have to relive the losing of their limbs time after time, day after day, until the director is satisfied. I feel like Lloyd asking, 'And tell me, how does it feel?'

Running alongside the gift of communicating with a live audience was a sense of being constantly thwarted. When we made a film of *Forever* for Television New Zealand in 1995 it was discovered, too late, that we couldn't afford the music rights. There was just enough for one showing and then, after one of the parties concerned heard

the work contained nudity and homosexuality, we were told we would be denied the rights to that particular piece of music forever, so to speak.

My life was devoted to making work and after 1990 I was operating with about half of the prodigious energy previously available. Outside work I barely existed, it was a sublimation. Then I was smitten by Sean, a Maori boy half my age who couldn't stop

smiling. Once I saw him walking in the rain, singing at the top of his

Male nakedness 'out of context'

WE can do without the disgusting performance of the Douglas Wright Dance Group (*Work Of Art, Forever*, TV1, May 28). It was slow, boring nonsense — people crawling semi-naked over one another, plus nude shower scenes. It was revolting and in bad taste. I hope kids who wish to become dancers don't have to see any more of this trash. It was a waste of Broadcasting Fee money.
FAME
(Auckland)

...I AM driven by sheer disgust to complain. If that is how our money is spent to see NZ On Air, I utterly deplore such a choice. The vulgarity of the 'dancing' scenes and showering in the nude, the display of male nakedness, was utterly out of context with dance as an art. The ridiculous *One Enchanted Evening* scenes were of debauchery and violence. Is this what NZ calls art? What proportion of us enjoy this gratuitous vulgarity?
BARBARA M. (Auckland)

Forever 'best dance in years'

AFTER it had started, I flicked the channel buttons and discovered *Forever* (*Work Of Art*, TV1, May 28). I was instantly enchanted by the subtle forms of the graceful dance routine and became mesmerised as the tale unfolded. Except for a few slips in precision, it was the best dance I have seen in years and the images were embedded in my memory. The letters in *TV Guide* (June 9) condemning the free-expression (dance has always been free of inhibition!) have both saddened me and turned me scribe. I did not find this erotic or embarrassing as maybe Fame or Barbara M did. And why did they? The second most erotic form of

dancing is called ballet! It started life with the intention of titillation but, due to its antiquity and quality, we call this band of males and females, culture. Aficionados always describe their love of ballet as the grace of movement, not the semi-nudity of the performers. So why pick on this troupe? Quite simply the complainers did not understand the beauty of movement. When they get to see some old, culturally acceptable ballet, they will really be shocked! Protesters should discover that hiding the body is a lot more enticing (disgusting according to Fame) than exposure.
JOHN DONNY (Auckland)

voice and smiling at the same time. He was dazzling, and the raindrops on his cheeks made him look as if not only was he singing and smiling, but he was also crying as he walked. I captured him for a while. But I had no energy to give him and after two years we broke up.

I danced less and less but when I did it made me happy. After 20 years I was just beginning to be able to transform the shit of my fear into gold when my body said enough. My relationship with the audience, which began at primary school, was even more primary by the time I danced myself to a standstill. When a dancer reaches the stage where they can stop thinking about technique, something else comes into play. Some people believe the dancing body is an instrument of the intellect. For me, the choreography, the music and the people watching were all ingredients in a journey I took every time I danced in public. At times I felt like a being set free in an enchanted sphere, one wing despair, the other – jubilation; plundering the gaps between the notes where the nectar is, with the watching gazes somehow fused into one giant eye, drinking. And what the audience drank was absorbed, enriched and purified by their understanding, then sent back to me. This mysterious give and take, back and forth went on and on until it was no longer clear exactly who was watching and who was dancing.

After a while I only ever danced one dance, despite the different steps. It was an odd process, not wholly explicable. Hours before the performance an image or a phrase would appear in my head and all day I'd let my mind nibble on it, gently, in a kind of daydream. Later, just before going on, the concentration would narrow and deepen. Then, once started, I stopped thinking altogether and let my body milk the metaphor, using it as fuel for a kind of self-hypnosis, the inducing of a state where there was no doubt in my mind I was dancing with and for something omnipotent. Life *and* death. I had full-blown delusions of grandeur and self-annihilation. It was heaven. One phrase I used was 'Christ the tiger', to help envisage a ferocious sweetness.

Of course it wasn't always like that. Sometimes everything was slightly off, and all I could think about was what came next and how I was about to forget it, but even then I knew I was doing what I was meant to. I suppose the stage was the only place I ever really felt in my element. Even now I've stopped, I'm a ghost dancer.

Driving around car-throttled Auckland I often find myself shaking my head at what other drivers do and lately I've started to see other drivers doing it too. That movement reminds me of the movement dancers make in rehearsal when they want to let you know that they know they've just made a mistake. It's an odd little movement, like a blinkered horse whinnying, and it tries to shake off criticism and attract praise. The small proportion of dancers addicted to it need to be broken of the habit because if not they start shaking their heads at themselves automatically, even in performance, and I imagine in other more private moments. Actually it's such an expressive gesture, so revealing and deliciously annoying I almost want to take it home and do something with it.

– 20 –

The marriage of left and right

Over the years the left side of my body has borne the brunt of all the wild flingings the stronger right side has initiated. I've had a broken left leg, left arm, left collarbone, left toe, and sustained an injury on the left side of my upper-middle back, where the wing once was. These days a constant gnawing pain has its roots just under the left-bottom edge of the helmet of my skull. It connects in intermeshing ramifications up into my left eye, down the neck to the ripped wing, and on into the tributary of my left arm. I feel that if I could somehow slice myself clean in half vertically down the centre, replicate my right side, then join the two right sides together I'd be free of the pain that haunts me. In my search to appease the nagging left side I spent years being massaged, chiropracted, therapied and

once went to a woman who encouraged me to let the left side tell the right how it felt. After its tale of being unappreciated and bullied I was then urged to let the right side thank the left for all the work it had done and to say how sorry it was to have caused any injury. Then the two sides made friends. As a gesture of goodwill I even allowed the left side of my body to initiate the movement vocabulary for an entire dance, *Arc*. But the alliance didn't last and the pain still rages, muffled slightly by the little white pills I take every four hours.

It seems to me that the right side of my body is the conqueror and the left the conquered; the right my father, the left my mother. Sometimes in meditation I can feel the left side being nourished, like a wilting plant being watered. And when I walk in the park amongst the massive trees, I like to touch and even whisper to them. I'm careful not to let anybody see me but I feel the trees are aware of me and welcome my attention. I don't think I'm the only one guilty of tree-fondling. I change my course so the leaves stroke my head as I pass. It's so soothing; I don't know why but the trees make the left side hurt less. They fill me with quiet. Some of them have trunks that divide into two, equal-sized branches and these trees look, to me, like the inverted legs, crotch and torso of giant nymphs,

dryads, diving headlong into the earth.

When I came to live in my unit in 1992, the garden was completely empty except for an arthritic lemon. In between making dances I absentmindedly planted trees that are now a dense green forest darned and mended by swift-threading birds. The kauri is virile, the rimu laments, the Chatham Island nikau is my totem. It has a fleshy pale-mauve flower like branches of coral. There's a crab-apple with red fruit that longs to be eaten and in summer vivid outlawed parrots descend on it in flocks, tobogganing down the branches, swearing and cracking jokes in their broad Australian accents. Palms, to me, are royal, their trunks spurt and gush in fountains of green; the mammoth magnolia goes from bride to widow and then back to bride, eternally hopeful and eternally bereft. I planted a cycad to attract dinosaurs, and cacti for their endurance; they remind me of Butoh dancers, moving so slowly that when they flower, it's like a startling image that snuck up on you, then opened its bearded petals in 'the room two inches behind the eyes'. Spiders weave their webs on the cacti, over the valleys, between the prickles. We co-exist. I've given up trying to get rid of them; besides, I admire their diligence. I saw one the other day. I was out in the garden

looking up and the spider was climbing a single thread that, because of the way the light fell, was invisible. The spider was climbing the sky.

A few years ago Housing New Zealand installed smoke alarms throughout my unit but they turned out to be faulty. Over a period of about six months, for no apparent reason, one by one they all began screaming in the dead of night and no matter what I did they wouldn't stop. Each time it happened I wrapped the alarm in blankets and put it on the balcony but I could still hear its wail, so in exasperation I threw them like frisbees in the direction of the stream and the golf course, so I could get some sleep. A month or so after I got rid of the last one I heard a screech that sounded familiar and when I looked out I saw a family of pukeko clawing at each other like enraged drag queens on the banks of the stream. Two of them fell into the water in a skirmish of red beaks, royal blue plumage and prehensile feet, either fighting or making love, I couldn't tell which. The others ran up and down the bank urging them on in falsetto. Their piercing cries were so similar to the smoke detectors I was struck by the absurd idea that the alarms had turned into the pukekos and were still trying to warn me. The pukekos live in uneasy harmony with flotillas of ducks and two fat, subconscious eels. Leo thinks them all unutterably ridiculous, and too big to kill.

When I go out in the garden Leo always follows; he runs and jumps and writhes on his back in rapture, then lifts his tail and squirts a thin stream of fluid onto each corner to let everyone know it's his. If I start dancing he sits and looks at me in amazement; once he taught me an exquisite movement that, apparently, I am the first non-cat to ever master. In the early days, when he had 'ballon', I once saw him jump the creek, which bank to bank, must be ten feet. I wondered what he was doing, nervously pacing on the bank, measuring the distance in his head, and then he jumped at exactly the moment I realised he was going to. It seemed impossible, and at the height of his arc he hung in the air, like Nijinsky, for an instant almost motionless, as if he was about to plummet into the creek, but then he sailed on and made it easily to the other side, stalking off to torture rats without a backward glance. Now his jumping days are over, but he still gets frisky. If I show visitors around the garden he likes to skite, and now that he's slightly rotund, the way he gallops uphill makes him blush. But he can't help it, just the same way I can't help playing Patti Smith.

I can hear generations of flatmates echoing down the years. 'Oh no, not Patti Smith again.' Patti Smith is the New York singer and poet who started a revolution. I first heard her music in 1975, downstairs in Music City, the record shop I had just been fired from. When I dropped in to visit, one of my ex-coworkers said, like a diagnosis, 'You better listen to this,' and handed me 'Horses', her first album. I put the headphones on and gazed at the photograph on the cover as, after a mournful piano intro, a deep boy-girl voice intoned, 'Jesus died for somebody's sins, but not mine.' As I listened the voice unleashed a tornado which picked me up and whirled me to a place I'd never been, then out of nowhere set me back down with a sneer, a purr and a whisper. I stared at the photograph on the cover with the same intensity I used to stare at the photographs of Janet and Nijinsky – the same stare I later used for looking at the only known photograph of Emily Dickinson.

Patti Smith, photographed by Robert Mapplethorpe. Skinny and elongated, black hair crackling with energy like live wires or snakes, she stared back at me with a defiant calm. Posed against a shadowy white wall like a Modigliani lounge-lizard in a white shirt and black trousers, a jacket slung over her shoulder, mouth brimming with transgressions, a wing of light resting on her shoulder. Now I had the album at home in St George's Bay Road in Parnell and was smacked out, lying down, listening to it. I was anaesthetised and this time Patti Smith performed an operation on me. Her voice made the incision, then entered; wringing its hands, gnashing its teeth, cradling, begging, taunting, getting down on its knees and keening, and then at the end her voice was even kind of friendly as it sewed me back up again. I became a Patti Smith fanatic. There is something primal about her; she inspires extremes. The mayhem in her voice and her androgynous image remind me of those youths in ancient Dionysian cults who, in the frenzy of purification rituals, sometimes ran to the centre of the temple space, took off their clothes, and with a sword which was put there for that purpose, immediately castrated themselves. According to the second century AD Grecian writer Lucias, these devotees then ran through the city holding in their hands their severed genitals, taking female clothing and women's adornments from whichever house they threw them into. After that they lived and worked as women, worshipping the Goddess.

Between 1975 and 1980 Patti Smith released four albums and I listened to them religiously, in the same way perhaps as ancient soothsayers studied the flight of birds to determine the future. I felt she was transmitting a message to me which could be summed up in the word *courage*. By the time I got to New York, Patti Smith had moved to Detroit with her husband to raise a family. She stopped recording. It was as if she had died and her absence from the streets I now wandered underlined for me the gap between my wild, lost years and my newfound vocation. But her voice was imprinted on me and when she resurfaced in 1996 after a series of bereavements, I was elated. Her new work is full of compassion and her voice has deepened and thickened. But she still roars like a lion, and no matter what she sings, I listen.

Chloe is another friendly Smith. I first met her when I was a dancer in Limbs and she was the assistant-manager. I always think of Chloe as having a shock of bright-red hair, even though these days it's black and short. We are both missing a few layers of skin, share a love of animals and have conversations that start, 'Just between you and me.' When she worked on *Xena – Warrior Princess* and *Hercules*, Chloe helped me to live, and when Patti Smith came to Auckland to open for Bob Dylan in 1998, Patti's daughter, Jesse, wanted to visit the set of *Xena*. When asked, Chloe, being very quick on the draw, replied, 'Only if you take my friend Douglas backstage to meet Patti Smith.' And that's how after seeing my idol perform for the first time after 23 years of devotion, I found myself in a room backstage at the North Shore Convention Centre, waiting for her.

Onstage she had been all I imagined, her physical mannerisms perfectly matching the aural ones I had etched in my brain. Even though I retained my genitals, seeing her 'live' was like finding the last fragment of a broken vessel, putting it together, filling it with water and drinking. In the few minutes before she came out I felt I was about to meet one of the famous dead, like Arthur Rimbaud or Emily Dickinson. And when the door opened I was initially taken aback at her zombie-ness. On stage she exuded love and a warm, raunchy charisma but up close her skin was grey and battered, her eyes had pin-prick pupils and one of them veered alarmingly off to the side, like a horse panicking. She was in her early fifties then but it wasn't age I was looking at, it was as if I was meeting the triumphant personification of the world's leftsidedness. A Tantrika. Her voice was so deep and croaky she sounded like she was channelling William Burroughs, the dead sheriff. 'Pleased ta meetya.' We shook hands and I babbled like an idiot. She was kind and told me how she'd wet her pants on stage, asking of her performance, 'Was it okay?' We wandered off to the side together as she signed my book of her poems. Patti was shod in the biggest, clompiest, many-strapped and buckled boots in existence and had the air of the grandest bullshitter that ever lived, yet at the same time was the wounded healer, the Sufi mistress, with her torn hem of a voice and raven hair. We had our picture taken together and I told her that without her, my own work would never have been. We laughed at something and I caught a glimpse of the little girl inside the black

widow. When I left Patti, she took my hand and dropped a gawky curtsy, then disappeared, bootbells ringing, into the Ladies.

That first night my seat was near the front so when she came out,

FREE WORLD
DANCIN'
DONT SAY NOTHING
BECAUSE THE NIGHT
GHOST DANCE
SOUTHERN CROSS
DEAD CITY
ABOUT A BOY
PEOPLE
R&R NIGGER

I joined the rush of fans to dance at the lip of the stage. I'd forgotten people did that but it was fun, seeing her up close, dancing to the music, ignoring the cries of 'Sit down!' 'Fuck off!' 'We can't see!' I went to the show again the next night, exhausted from my encounter with the diva, and my seat was upstairs, miles from the stage. When Patti came on, the thirtyish male-female couples around me kept talking. They were there to see Bob Dylan. They chatted all through her set and at one point one of the women bleated to her boyfriend, 'She's not bad,' and he grunted. I was too timid to ask them to shut up. Then when Patti improvised some poetry over an undulating sea of sound, with a tambourine in her hand, a male voice rose up out of the downstairs crowd. 'Get off!' he yelled. But Patti didn't even blink; she was up to 'the sky's opera' and no punk was going to distract her. Billie shares my love of Patti Smith and often when I lived with him we 'had a little smokette' and listened to 'Horses' or 'Radio Ethiopia'. Recently, when I told him about my headaches, Billie was very sympathetic and related, over the phone, how his own terrible migraines had been cured. He was in hospital for a hernia operation when an old nurse – 'a horrible old woman, I was frightened of her' – came in and said she had come to shave Esmeralda. Billie said, 'Oh, what room is she in?' and the woman said, 'She's here, down there,' pointing at his crotch. 'Back with the blankets.' Billie said, 'No way you're touching me!' but then some other nurses appeared like a flock of screaming gulls and they held him down, started to soap up all around that area and then shaved off his pubic hair. 'All that business down there shrivelled up with fright. It was filthy,' Billie said, 'and the other nurses were peering round the corner giggling.' As the old nurse walked out she called out to Billie over her shoulder, 'Never mind, they'll all grow back nice and black and curly.'

'And, do you know, Douglas,' Billie said, 'without a word of a lie, up until that time I had the most TERRIBLE migraines you can imagine, I was eating Codral sandwiches. But when those harpies did that to me, I got such a shock I've never had a migraine since, not a twinge.'

My father must have got wind of my disgusting relationship with a man older than him because once when I was living with Billie and we were driving home in the white Jaguar I saw him, in his shorts, walking up the hill. I dived to the floor of the car and when we got home we locked ourselves in and refused to answer the door. By that time my father had started a new family with his Maori partner, Rau. I've since met her, once or twice, and my three handsome step-brothers. I liked Rau; she was gentle and welcoming and my father seemed happy, still drinking home-brew and watching the footy. But we had nothing, or too much, in common. There is a faint physical resemblance and the shared disease of an ancestral narcissism. My father's father is someone whose face I can't bring to mind. All I can see is him sitting on a chair with his back to the house next to his little shed, drinking beer and looking at his vegetable garden while I sat inside with Mum and Nana in the smoke-stained living-room, worrying. The only other memory I have of him is his funeral. Pop, as we called him, ran Tuakau Transport. He employed many local Maori and was well liked and respected by them. On the day of his funeral I discovered the local iwi had requested his body for a tangi on the Tuakau Marae. This was a great honour and the family accepted. First there was a Catholic service in the River Road Church; I hadn't been in since I abandoned the faith. The family tried to persuade Nana to stay at home because she was what they called over-emotional and they were afraid she'd try and throw herself in the grave. The only thing I remember about the Christian service was the door opening in the middle of it and Nana rushing in clutching a handkerchief. She was tiny and gnarled, with huge streaming eyes, and didn't seem to know where to put herself, like a bird trapped in a house. At the marae, the Maori sang us on as we walked behind the coffin. I don't remember what happened, people spoke I suppose, but I can still see the old Maori ladies dressed in black, the green ferns under the scarves on their heads intertwining with the green moko on their chins, and feel the river of grief flowing where before, in the church, it had been dammed.

Nana Wright went downhill after that; she became senile and was put in a home. Mum told me recently that Nana had once been a beauty queen; she was Miss Tuakau 1925 and had always kept her hair permed and neat, but in the old people's home it had gone straight and hung down in rags. Mum took me to see her when I was back for a holiday from New York, but she thought I was someone else and was busy tearing a copy of the *Woman's Weekly* into tiny pieces, and died after I'd gone back.

Mum's parents were Presbyterians and were dead against her marrying my Catholic father. She had to leave home when she got engaged to him and they had nothing to do with her for a year. She tells me that she and my father went to several discussions with the priest while they were engaged, and because she didn't 'turn' Catholic there was no music at my parents' wedding. They both had to sign a paper promising all their children would be christened Catholic. Nana and Granddad Johansen came round in the end, after they'd seen the house Mum and Dad built in readiness. But they

never liked my father and barely knew his parents. So it's a curious fact that, by accident, all four of my grandparents, the Wrights and the Johansens, are buried together, next to each other, in the Tuakau Cemetery. They are buried in double plots, with the grandfathers at the bottom, side by side, and the grandmothers, likewise, on top. I can't help wondering how this bizarre coincidence came about and how Nana Johansen felt when she saw, at Granddad's funeral, who they were next to for eternity.

23/24 Aug the timing (2002)

Dearest Douglas

This is all good for you and your family and whoever else is in your entourage. So tis difficult to pick up on anything or nothing or everything. Sorry that cannot seem to cope with all that is going on. Bill Weaver sends all good   , too. The good Lord knows that I want to be certain that I am going on my way to nothing but beautiful singing of days of your. I don't have my nephews need longer but surely the people that worship the might mighty dollar. I can hardly set anything to music, so much music to be listening. You see the men and their families. You can see and feel that I am not up to my normal way of living. So off the wall. Nothing real or unreal is going to destroy what the people, the radio continues for many days. I cannot listen and comment. Even the cards that Floriano makes are looking great! It's driving me crazy. I am ready to ask questions of myself. How are you feeling? (in the voice of any of the great singers of the marvellously exciting), exhilarating CDs that the met has done. Having nothing to say is a bit cuckoo for me but worse is that I have no beginning to the great classics.

Much love,
      Tobias

Dammit! But I miss you!

– 21 –

Albatross!

On the third and final day of our previously described visit to Dunedin, Malcolm and I drove around the coast to visit the albatross colony at Taiaroa Head. When we arrived we climbed the concrete steps to a building with a plaque outside informing us that Princess Anne, the Princess Royal, had officially opened the colony in 1989. Inside it was like the waiting-room for an upmarket high-security prison. We tried to find a way to walk up to the rocky crag which was visible above the building but discovered a fortress of high fences with padlocks and lines of tourists waiting for the guided tour. They looked at us as if we were queue-jumping so we retreated back into the pastel waiting-room, mumbling, 'Fuck this.' There was a café with a large window that looked out onto the area where the famous seabirds were supposedly kept free from harassment. Several people sat at tables with their coffee looking out, and every now and then a woman standing in the corner in a uniform called out in a loud monotone, 'Albatross!' and then the heads of the watching people swivelled to catch sight of the bird as it flew past. 'Albatross!' she yelled as their heads swivelled back, 'Albatross!' as we hurried out past the gift-shop with albatross mugs, tee-shirts, tea-towels, ornaments, posters, books, videos and postcards. Malcolm says he glimpsed the bird itself but I didn't see it.

Rather than go back the same way we decided to drive over the hills. Just as we were entering the fog we saw a McCahon through the trees, a faithful copy of one of his early landscapes. Then the fog thickened until I couldn't even see the road in front of us. I slowed the car to walking pace. It was like being bandaged from head to foot; there was no sound, no wind. We were stranded in a warm bubble on a tranquil white sea, wrapped in white fog, anaesthetised.

Huge black macrocarpa trees loomed, floated past like octopuses and were swallowed up. A sign in the shape of an arrow materialised with the word *Castle* written on it and we laughed. At one point I thought we'd stopped moving altogether then a rear view of a lone cyclist appeared in front of us and slowly pedalled backwards past the car as we overtook him. He looked as if he was being dragged by an undertow, or a macrocarpa tentacle, and as he disappeared into the fog, like the last fugitive thought before white-out, I saw the look of horror on his face as he struggled to breathe.

– 22 –

Battalion of angels

So much for the past. Now I'm back to where I departed from. The posthumous feeling hasn't faded, there's just a different light on it now, as if I got so far behind, everybody else caught up. I feel like someone who has worn the same thing for years, never deserting the style of their youth until, after being passé for decades, they fleetingly find themselves the height of fashion. These days, in England, there are people who pay to watch autopsies live, so to speak. Death is now 'in'. Whenever I turn on the television after a day wrestling with words there's a dead body undergoing a post-mortem or a team of forensic investigators swarming over murdered corpses. In between wisecracks they follow the trail of hair, fibre, saliva, tears, mucus, excrement, semen, skin cells and fingerprints that leads from the victim to the culprit, with DNA as their lasso. They also identify and measure any insects that have set up house in the cadaver, to determine time of death. These flies and sometimes ants devote their entire existence to assisting the process of decomposition, cleaning bones of rotting flesh, then polishing them. Ants live in colonies, and have a caste system, like humans. The trails of innumerable workers, to and from the queen's nest, are a common sight. Driving around Auckland, crawling on my wheels, I sometimes wonder if the human race is unwittingly performing the same function as these insects, each of us carrying between our metal mandibles a tiny bite of the dead city back to our lairs to eat. And if I happen to be walking there is always a car-armoured human impatiently waiting to go wherever I am or making me wait as they get there first. From this perspective the cars are less insect and more like cornered bulls on the verge of a dangerous panic. It makes me wish I had one of those working dogs farmers use to help round up their cattle and sheep.

When I was a child I used to spend every second weekend with Nana and Granddad, Mum's parents, on their farm at Te Kohanga. Cecil and Ruby Johansen had a hill the shape of a lion which, so Mum told me, was called Kaitangata or Eatman, and they spoke in special farming voices, echoing the animals they tended. They worked from dawn till dusk and when we rounded up the sheep Granddad's dogs knew exactly what he meant by his piercing whistles, and barked and growled commands. They crawled on their bellies, sneaking up on the stragglers, then ran like lightning at a signal. Sometimes if a lamb lost its mother Nana would bring it in out of the cold and sit it in the lap of the oven, to keep it warm, leaving the door open. I always laughed at that. At the end of a long, hard day everyone was so tired we just ate politely and Granddad fell asleep over the newspaper while Nana knitted and peered over her glasses at us. Their clock had a loud tick and bonged the hours.

But I don't think the cars would take any notice of a shepherd or his dogs. I know if I was behind the wheel I'd toot my horn and shake my head and curse with impatience. After a day in the city it's oddly comforting to think that perhaps one day all trace of our predation will be wiped clean and this isthmus will be given back to the volcanoes, the ravening sky and the sea.

On my daily walks I regularly pass a building site in the various stages of construction. There are walls being knocked down by violent machines and other machines with metal proboscises that ram deeply satisfying holes in the ground. Rooms that look like archaeological digs, excavations of sodden clay, with concrete steps leading to and from nowhere stand next to wooden skeletons through which you can see the sky. Sometimes it's difficult to tell whether they are building something or dismantling it. For the last year or so there have been increasingly urgent reports of thousands of houses in the country that are leaking and rotting. Since the abolition of compulsory timber treatment in 1996 houses are being built with untreated *pinus radiata* in flimsy 'mediterranean' styles. In an interview on the radio the head of the Leak Investigation Committee seemed to be talking on a cellphone as he walked on tiptoe through a dissolving building. His voice kept breaking up into metallic molecules and hurricanes of static. Through the inter- ference he sounded, in sepulchral tones, a note of warning: 'This timber cannot tolerate even the most minor and normally acceptable degrees of moisture entry. We must always have an inherent background of durability to handle the minor ingress of water, which can never be prevented.' Some of the mould is toxic and causes diseases in humans.

Over the following weeks I listened as representatives of all the relevant authorities took refuge in a labyrinth of double-speak. The increasingly ornate figures of speech they used put me in mind of a story I once heard about a house that was haunted and needed to be kept in a continual state of construction to keep the ghost at bay. Its eccentric millionaire owner spent his entire life and fortune adding unnecessary rooms, chapels, flying buttresses, towers, staircases, conservatoria and miles of unwinding hallways to a house that was already finished. Apparently he died just after work on a new wing had got underway.

Malcolm and I mended our break, agreeing on the third person and an idiosyncratic syntax, and he is busy in cyberspace getting sidetracked, chasing Doratea down the years. I feel that through this search, he is somehow redeeming his mother from the last vestiges of blame. How could she have allowed his father to treat him that way? Her memory is being steeped in Doratea's compassion, in Pirimona's scrupulous conscience. It takes time.

Malcolm hated his parents with a pure and consuming hatred. I thought I knew how to hate but now I know I'm lucky to be a novice. To hate someone is like throwing a stone that never fails to somehow curve back on itself, or rebound and hit the thrower smack in the face. Scar tissue is numb. Just to trace the outline of Malcolm's story was like breathing on something frozen.

He still makes things and my unit is filled with his paintings and the sly objects he calls 'tutus'. Mostly we communicate by phone. There are two Malcolms. One is blurry and sentimental, the other dry and factual. They don't know each other very well and dislike it if I hold them to something the other has said or promised. The other day he said to me, 'I'm your feet of clay.' More recently I was surprised to discover the Maori concept of utu does not apply only to revenge for insults or wrongs inflicted, but also to reciprocating gifts and favours bestowed. Malcolm and I are slowly getting even.

Leo has decided to keep me on as a door-opener and supplier of portions of the herd of cattle he is gradually eating, so my days are full. When I'm lying on the couch reading or watching television he likes to settle on me. It must be marvellous to be a small living thing lying on a much larger living thing, like livestock in the folds of hills, or babies grazing on the flesh-pastures of the mother continent. Wanting in. It's a matter of trust. My mother and I still talk almost every night on the telephone. She long ago finished unravelling and re-knitting her cardigan and is now redoing the bathroom. But there is no end to the things to be done; it's more a matter of keeping up, of not getting too far behind. At the end of each conversation she always says with a sigh of regret, 'Oh well, I'd better let you go.'

Even though I rarely answer it when it rings, the telephone is my stethoscope. The other night it rang at about 4 a.m. and later that morning when I listened to the message it was Rick, my old friend, after 25 years, in Auckland on holiday. In a familiar slurring voice, he said he still loved me but was leaving the next morning to go back to his wife and stepchild in Australia. He had just been out to a nightclub and couldn't stop thinking of me so he called Billie to get my number. By the time I listened to the message it was too late; I'd just missed him.

This spring the primordial cycad had a flush of new growth and I keep a watchful eye for white-fly, small insects who like to suck the juice from the tender fronds. I spray them with a pesticide while overhead MAF planes and helicopters spray for another pest, the painted apple moth. The full effects of this chemical on humans is as yet unknown. On the six o'clock news every night the mother-and-father presenters are full of sinister warnings of biological weapons of mass destruction, bug spray for the human pest allegedly kept by fanatics who live somewhere else. War seems imminent. It's all so interconnected and confusing ... I suppose I should just let the white-fly eat the cycad.

These days when I'm out walking I've started to see faint, overgrown traces of other less frequented paths and now I take them. One such trail is in the park that the sheep use and there is another that leads from a busy main road to a graveyard. Here, a few feet away from the roaring traffic, there is an alternative city of marble grave-stones, urns, frozen angels and mausoleums in a pompous, grand style commemorating the rich who died in the nineteenth century. I scoured the place for anyone born in the 1700s and found just one. There are two moss- and lichen-covered tombstones inside a little wrought-iron fence with a crimson-flowering pohutukawa growing between and over them. With the passage of the years the roots of the tree have reached deep under the stones to push up and buckle the once-smooth bed of sleep so that the matching gravestones are now wildly askew, like two antique drunks holding each other up, the plums in their mouths turned to dust. In fact if you look carefully at all the various monuments they are none of them on the level, as if the dead had tried to send messages using their individual stones as pencils and had given up mid-sentence. Homeless people also hang out here, drinking their sherry in the sun on the wooden benches.

So far the voracious cars have steered clear of this graveyard with the unintended result that, despite the tilts, the cemetery contains some of the best architecture in the city.

It's summer now and the skeletons of the trees are clothed in green, making me think there may be a hereafter. Sometimes I hear murmured inklings of what comes next but they're so faint I can't decipher them. In my mind's eye I can see Tobias paddling away in the canoe of forgetting, Pirimona Te Kariri caught between two fires, and the nightingale on her fatal journey east. All around me I can sense the criss-crossing migrants and pilgrims, both accidental and deliberate, all affecting each other in ways as yet unknown, weaving our indivisible pattern. But ahead there's only a distant rumble, like an empty stomach, or the sound of forgiveness.

This indistinctness reminds me of something I saw one day in the studio when we were rehearsing *Gloria*. At the end of a tiring passage the dancers lay in two rows on their stomachs with their foreheads to the floor, legs together, arms palm down in crucifix position. After they got up I noticed they'd left, on the black linoleum, an X-ray image of their bodies, outlined in sweat. And as I watched the battalion of spectral angels flying towards me, they slowly evaporated.

Afterword

Six and a half weeks after I finished writing this book Malcolm died from a bewilderingly ferocious and invasive cancer. It happened so quickly, there was less than twenty-four hours between the final diagnosis and his death. I was one of a small group which included his brother Duncan that was with him in the Intensive Care Unit at Whangarei Hospital when he died. By that time he was unconscious, slowly choking, and as the exhausted tide of breath went further and further out, Mel, one of what he called 'my old Maori ladies', touched him oh so gently on the head.

'That's right, Malcolm,' she said. 'Go on then, straight to Mum.'

And so he went, and now I want, more than anything, to tell him all the things that happened next.

List of Illustrations

All choreography by Douglas Wright unless otherwise noted.

Douglas Wright was born in Tuakau, South Auckland in 1956. He danced with Limbs Dance Company of New Zealand, the Paul Taylor Company of New York and DV8 Physical Theatre of London before forming the Douglas Wright Dance Company in 1989. His works include: *Knee Dance*, *Faun Variations*, *Hey Paris*, *How on Earth*, *Gloria*, *Elegy*, *Forever*, *Buried Venus*, *halo*, *Arc* and *Inland*.

In 2000 he was one of the five inaugural Arts Foundation of New Zealand Laureates and in 2003 was the subject of a feature-length documentary film, *Haunting Douglas*, directed by Leanne Pooley.